Praise for W. S. Di Piero

Mallarmé said the poet's job is to purify the language of the tribe. W. S. Di Piero does just that, mainly by aligning his rich, working class memories with a larger world of art and politics.

—Library Journal

W. S. Di Piero is probably the most consisten~~~ ~~~'ing and idiosyncratic prose writer among contemp~~~ ~~~oets.

etry

Like other young intellectua~~~ ~~~g the 1960s, Di Piero returns repeatedly to ~~~ ~~~oads of literature and politics, to what he calls "a pa~~~ ~~~.errogation of history and memory."

—The Washington Post

W. S. Di Piero is one of the most bracing critical intelligences now at work in our national scene of writing.

—The Boston Book Review

Mickey Rourke
and the
Bluebird of Happiness

Other works by W. S. Di Piero

Poetry

The First Hour (1982)
The Only Dangerous Thing (1984)
Early Light (1985)
The Dog Star (1990)
The Restorers (1992)
Shadows Burning (1995)
Skirts and Slacks (2001)
Brother Fire (2004)
Chinese Apples: New and Selected Poems (2007)
Nitro Nights (2011)
TOMBO (2014)
The Man on the Water (2017)

Essays

Memory and Enthusiasm: Essays 1975-1985 (1989)
Out of Eden: Essays on Modern Art (1991)
Shooting the Works: On Poetry and Pictures (1996)
City Dog (2009)
When Can I See You Again: New Art Writings (2010)

Translations

Pensieri, Giacomo Leopardi (1981)
This Strange Joy: Selected Poems of Sandro Penna (1982)
The Ellipse: Selected Poems of Leonardo Sinisgalli (1982)
Ion, Euripides (1996)

Mickey Rourke

and the

Bluebird of Happiness

⌒

A Poet's Notebooks

W. S. Di Piero

Carnegie Mellon University Press

Pittsburgh 2017

Acknowledgments

Some of the material in this book appeared in some form in three previous collections: *Memory and Enthusiasm* (Princeton University Press), *Out of Eden* (University of California Press), and *Shooting the Works* (TriQuarterly Books). Some material also appeared in various periodicals: *Threepenny Review*, *Poetry*, *TriQuarterly*, *Manoa*, and *Zyzzyva*.

Thanks in particular to certain editors who have been steadfast for so long: Wendy Lesser, Christian Wiman, and Reginald Gibbons.

Book design by Danielle Lehmann

Library of Congress Control Number 2017937499
ISBN 978-0-88748-624-1
Printed and bound in the United States of America

10 9 8 7 6 5 4 3 2 1

Contents

From the 2000s

If you live a long time with chronic pain, when the levels spike it helps to have a map. Tonight I imagine my body as a night sky, and certain stars are hot spots. They constellate to form a picture, a self-portrait. Star light, star bright.

—

Daylight Saving Time. Late day, sunlight breaks into the kitchen but along the way diffuses into powdered ores on my unwashed windows. Yesterday, a fat faintly opaque moon like buff linen. In the a.m. the whiter light of morning spreads west across white buildings to the bluegray plateau of the Pacific. A raven's shadow wipes the rooftops.

—

Why the scenic in poetry matters: it *tells* the world (like telling a story) by saying how it looks, tastes, moves, smells. Tell the world well, even if it's an unhappy telling, and you reveal the invisible life of things.

—

Late in the p.m. I'm riding BART through its Bay waters tunnel, coming home from Berkeley, where whenever I emerge from the University Avenue station I feel culturally confused and morally disoriented. I'm surrounded by scolding righteousness and a class-motley nuttiness that comports itself as if it were exquisite entitlement. The speedy angry wheelchairs, the ganja aromatics, the dopey cheer of crustpunks (and their pits and rotts), the streetfolk indistinguishable from grad students—that University Avenue corner induces a vaguely precious congestive disgust and primes me to find even more disgraceful than usual the *other* Berkeley where I'd just been, the tamped-down, monied gentility of College Avenue, where good behavior is on its best behavior. So I'm happy to be going home to San Francisco, when a young woman sits next to me. "Excuse me, sir. Sir? Can I ask you something?" Hard to guess her age. Anglo, heavy-bodied, sweaty, pimples disfiguring her nose and forehead, nicely dressed, but she stinks of piss. "Sir? Tell me, if you *knew* somebody was going to die tonight. I mean you *knew* it, and you knew *when*. And you *know* the person. What would you *do*?" Whose life? Anyone's *real* life? Does she really want an answer? A solution? My existence on earth in an instant contracts to our shared seat. Any words that might pass between us, beyond what she has said, are fraught with urgent intimacy. My head feels pressured by the water around the tunnel our train is pushing through. The sea, my home sea, is just down the street.

⌇

Poetry is cellular matter, connective tissue, interstitial stuff, not skeletal. "Life," writes a friend, "is lived in its transitions." Thus the fatigue of writing: it comes from sustaining that awareness of a life that never quite arrives or leaves.

⌇

How I love Schiele. His *Sunflowers* is nature as root cellar, drab greens and browns, all snotty effluvial color, the blooms sickened, failing, and in the middle sky a sun blanched of its fires, its sunfloweriness.

⌇

Christmas in Taos, *luminarias* everywhere—the most sensual light, honey with a pulse. The full moon turns fresh snow into moonlight. Christmas Eve ceremony in the Pueblo. Muddy ice-mounded ground where bonfires large and small fire up sparks and charcoal smoke. A father shows his young son how to pluck a firebrand from the shaggy ends of piñon pine splittings then passes the brand to the child so he can light other parts of the pile. We live into the layers of our stories, as deeply as we can. Into shared myths. Meleager's mother, told by the Fates that he'd live only until fire consumed a burning brand, pulled the stick from the fire, put it out and hid it. Meleager kills her brothers in some dispute. The mother returns the brand to the fire.

⌣

Poetry as a raised voice? Most good poems are serial sounds in pursuit of a shapely sense. If the Orphic is forfeited and poetry's vocalizing—sounds made for no more purpose than birdsong or wind in leaves—diminishes, poetry becomes a conceptualizing activity, and it's that conceptualizing, the music of mentality, that seems to predominate now and override desires for sonorities, mouth-feel, chromatics, dissonance, tempi, etc.

⌣

I thought of it as chapel time, because in my childhood heart it was a cloistered chamber where a supreme voice spoke stories to the one person present, me, who meant the most. Chapel time at night between my mother and me took place with a casual ceremonialism while I lay in bed and she read stories till it was time to sleep. *Goodnight Moon*, *Peter Rabbit*, *Winnie*, a chopped-down *Pinocchio*, *Curious George*. Later came longer sessions with fables and King Arthur tales while I stayed awake to ride the current, because a book, especially in the dry stage whisper my mother favored, wasn't just an episode or anecdote, it was *story*, a weave of dreamy urgent fact that moved in an imagined time, repeated so often that I memorized phrases even though every reading felt like a nonce moment. I most loved hearing the first of Walter R. Brooks's *Freddy the Pig* series (which I eventually took over on my own, all 23 books). The narratives were so embedded in the rhythms of the sentences and the playful urgency of my mother's voice that I was barely aware of the sense of things. Yet everything made sense. When I try to imagine what it might be like not to have been read to, I cannot even think the thought.

⌣

Here's another poetry. At the end of a radio interview, the sound engineer tells me to be silent so he can get "some room tone." (The room had more to say than I did.)

⌣

What if death is just another country of contingency, contingency we can't imagine, so we have to believe it's an empire of pure necessity. Then imagine death not as a state, not non-being, but a condition where consciousness is free in a way that it cannot be free in life.

⌣

Nothing I said about chapel time is true, except the fact that I read all the Freddy books on my own. It's my imagination of the scene and its sensations and life consequences, that secretiveness of story confided by parent to child. I wasn't read to. This isn't a woe-was-me moment, it's just how it was. There were virtually no books in the house (or neighborhood). I didn't read standard children's books until I read them to my daughter. My story life came mostly from Classics Illustrated, the Sears and Roebuck catalogs all my relatives seemed mysteriously to possess, and 1950s television, which was more cartoon or comic or superhero anecdote than story. I think probably TV cadences were planted deeper and earlier in me than sentence-by-sentence tempo, earlier than written time. The evening protocol in our house was that at a certain hour I was sent to bed, good night & good luck. Which may have been a good thing, since in the silence where a voice might have been, I invented complex stories in which I made myself the shining though sometimes suffering hero. (One involved a host of small, angry, man-eating crabs emerging from the sea to chew on my feet while, lashed to a post, I suffered but endured.) Is the voice a companion and a vehicle of love, even though we can't know what that really is when it's happening? When I finally acquired, at age eight or nine, a library card, my pass to millions of words in impeccable orders, I was, without quite knowing it, primed by lack.

⌣

You can hate facts but not resent them.

14

I'm at the Green Mill in Chicago, listening to Patricia Barber and her quartet. They're into "Cherokee," but not the standard tom-tom swing rendition. Patricia's husky whisper of the lyrics retards everything. It feels as if time itself is slowing down while she finds her way through the music. I've seen her and her boys several times, and one of the pleasures is watching them converse with each other through the music, talking, in their way, about time and how it's passing. There are pauses, intervals when everything stops, they all look at each other, then jump back in, laughing. Music is about the motion of existence we try to measure by calling it time. It's the completed incomplete. Poetry may create its own time signature but a text is a text, a codification that binds up time. Musicians take themselves out of time in order to *work* it, as if time were material kneaded, stretched, shoved around, squeezed, and we listeners feel time passing through us.

A critic writes that my poetry fails to see and speak of "the general human condition." That generality is self-evident. What's not is the cellular specificity of a fact of a life as it's lived and laid momentarily to rest in a recognizable yet somehow strange pattern of words. I'm not interested in being sententious or ruminative. I want to say small things intensely.

I go to an SFMOMA exhibition of Ólafur Elíasson's work. He turns out wiry, boxy, ropy rhomboids, helixes, gyroscopic concoctions. In one gallery they were spread on the floor, shelved up and down the walls—it looked like the overstuffed room of an entitled child. And there were environments—light, depth, cold, a sensation of running water. They're intended to teach us to experience our surround with greater acuity. But our surround usually just happens to us, it befalls us, or else we find ourselves in it and find something fresh there (or not). Elíasson's art manipulates us into artificial wonder. It comes at us, it doesn't invite (or patiently wait for) us to come to it. It envelops, it interprets itself on our behalf. Then there's art as a greeting—

an intense, complex, astonishing greeting. I left the museum and walked to Yerba Buena gardens, where a Cuban band was working it up—joyful art-making, process *and* effect, and vital. *And* the joy of communal ecstatic dance is darkly threaded with anarchic terror, and anarchic unreasoning hope.

⌣

To write a poem that's a sustained concentrate of feeling and that's at the same time *about* that condition, that effort to live intensely, write intensely, and not be able to tell the difference.

⌣

The bed-time book-time intimacy I *do* know is that of reading to lovers. The resonating tissue of the speaking voice and the some-thing spoken, shared, is so sexual, one more extension of sensation and rapture. Lamplight, air somehow scented with cedarwood (soap? shampoo? hallucinated sensation?) warm feet, mercy & safety in bed, and a chapel voice pronouncing a liturgy for just us two initiates. I've always been the reader, so I wonder how it is to fall asleep to a quiet storytelling voice, until nothing thought can be told apart from the words on their way to other words that smear into dream-streaming or contented oblivion.

⌣

Fat Tuesday then Ash Wednesday. Runny pork fat chased by dry charred atonement. An excess of ashes is as inviting as an excess of meat and beads and bacon grease. Poetry treads water in the stream of the process, wet to dry, fat to dust, superfluity to barely surfeit. In my childhood the ashy forehead smudge was more a mark of fallenness than sign or promise of rebirth. We were already—at eight years old—consigned to earth or urn. What had we children done to cause this to be required of us?

⌣

Dreams are the deranged, disguised partners of our clarified waking mental life. A recent twosome:

1. A young Asian woman walking with a much older man like me but not me, their arms sexily around each other, the image rich with feeling of a lasting passion undeterred.

2. A neurologist shows me three sketches he's made of the interior of my skull; on each one, a mark indicates the same abnormality—"Priapism."

⌣

Riders on public transit bent to the shape of piety, ensorcelled by smart phone or iPad. The prayer beads of our time. Checking, checking. How's the universe doing today?

⌣

Let us not forget. In the national spongy post-9/11 sympathy-fest, Southerners and Midwesterners were saying: "We're all New Yorkers now." They didn't remain New Yorkers very long. Most of the electorate living outside cities fears the uncontrollable diversity and hazards of big cities and hates how city culture seems to slight "family values" and good time religion. That improvised heartland solidarity was creepy, inauthentic, spoken with what James Baldwin called "an arid heart." Twelve months later it wasn't city folk who rallied behind the War in Iraq and the Good President who took us there.

⌣

On the street: "These are dime-store breasts. I wear them every day."

⌣

Back in Marfa and high-desert West Texas heat. Winds today at 30+ m.p.h. I'm accustomed to the sea wind in San Francisco—it's frontal, it comes *at* you. A windstorm here comes *for* you. It's a woman's voice hallooing right outside the door late tonight, trying to slither into the house and harmonize with the *Figaro* I'm listening to. It shimmies, it turns corners, it bullroars, in this otherwise silent place. How can you not believe that the wind carries the voices of the dead, long interred but now singing again for us to come to them and their sweet fine nothingness?

⌣

I think sleep is dreaming *me.* And in its dream, I'm awake at my familiar 4:00 a.m.

Dear sleep, for Christ's sake, wake up.

⌣

The body as a house of pain. No, check that. It's an airstream trailer of pain—an exquisite and completely practical streamlined availability, road-ready anytime anywhere.

⌣

Good art writers, rare ones like Baudelaire and John Berger, think or meditate not so much through pictures as *through life*, the life of appearances, thus life becomes some representation of itself. This renders interpretation aimless and inconsequential.

⌣

The country of contingency is full of rain.

⌣

In the Museum of Modern Art, my heart's adrift and achy with thoughts of young sons who lose their fathers, when I hear a guard (from the islands, from St. Vincent, it turned out) softly singing to himself what sounded like Gospel, and *was* Gospel, he said when I asked. The sound of song in public—doesn't matter if it's Gospel, rap, opera, tuneless humming—it thrills the air. (Today in a streetcar a high school kid improvised rhymes he was still putting down when I got off after several stops; as riders entered he worked into his song their clothes or shoes or belongings or skin type.) After that museum song came the formless sorrow I feel before one of Rothko's dark-smoky pictures, the nocturnal palette, always enchanting and unsettling, and I overhear a father tell his son how R's pictures were like windows and how you can see or imagine all sorts of feelings looking out windows, right? "He wasn't a happy man," he tells the boy. While I'm thinking about wisdom and tradition, R's mental agony, the hurt heart, I hear somebody call my name (sharply, like a cell phone dropped on a hard surface) but when I look around, nobody's there.

⌣

Overheard on the Boston "T": "Last night the devil was flicking his lighter in my lower intestine."

⌣

I've decided to sell off or give away most of my books. If I read them well in the first place, I'll always own them. They have certainly owned me, which is a reason for letting them go. I want them out of my apartment, out of my sight, and me out of *their* sight, for they've watched me—watched over and examined and compassed me—long enough. Time to go now, old friends, old obsessors, forsakers, forget-me-nots. Give me reprieve finally from that life of mind and heart that has come to oppress me. Time for you (and me) to go.

⌣

Francis Paudras, Bud Powell's caretaker and financial manager, kept the musician away from alcohol and drugs so that he could perform and record. During Powell's years in and out of institutions he said, "People think Bud is crazy or lost or silent, but he really is in a state of grace."

⌣

Aspirations. I wanted to write a poetry that enacted what it felt like to live in that impossible moment when a lived instant seems to recapitulate every previous instant—I wanted to engage consciousness as it lived into its own layers or zones. Reading all those books I've been selling off was as aspirational as it was instructive. And as a prettily pious Roman Catholic child I also muttered my way through who knows how many thousands of aspirations, brief devout utterances that were no more than a breath. A Catholic deacon of my generation, when I mention how the life aspirations that burned in my heart were very different from those other aspirations, says, "Let us not forget: they were also called ejaculations!"

⌣

I didn't know until a friend told me that if you squeeze a dried bunch of lavender the tickly sharp scent is released all over again. Pips that fall away can be gathered and bundled into sachets, squeezed again months later, and your head aches with memories you've not even recalled till now, the scent as piercingly fine as at the beginning. Certain pictures release the same kind of charge. The one I've lived with longest and has watched me over the arc of many years is a small self-portrait Tintoretto made at age twenty-three that hangs in Philadelphia. I saw it when I was twenty years old, and I only recently realized how I've clung to its presence as I've gone about the work of making my life. It's always the same but keeps changing up on me. I loved its brashness—T.'s over-the-shoulder stare says: Just watch what I can do. I forget the first astonishment until the second, which maybe won't occur for another ten years. Sometimes I'm looking at or for something else, or, as I change, the object wants different things from me. Years pass, sometimes I'm back in my home town, I always go right to the Tintoretto, and a freshness waits: *See what has become of me? I've never stopped desiring your attention.* When I saw it recently in a Boston show, it was the agitated reflection of a young artist trying to see into what he will, in fact, achieve. It restored my spirit to itself. But I also saw old man Master Tintoretto in the same picture; in that youthful, insolent head I saw a far-along life that never gave up exploration, process, renewal.

⌣

Another July Fourth. The familiar, dreary boom-booms and celestial whistles. How hopeful in a time of the most grotesque disparity between the rich and everybody else. The noise has nothing to do with hope. It's reflexive, uncurious American enthusiasm, a little stupid but so proudly unselfconscious that the stupidity is endearing. Tonight I didn't go floating through neighborhoods as I usually do. It would have only intensified and personalized the American forlornness of it all. O, fainthearted Fourth. O, freakout Fourth.

⌣

Writing about loss thrills and energizes because loss is another form of transformation—that's its grievous, dismal promise.

⌣

I meet a poet curious that I write so much prose, that I've written it for as long as I've written poetry, as if it were a subtropical, carnivorous plant. But I never knew any better. The poets I read early developed prose styles, so I took it on faith that a poet had to be a writer. It's best to do it mostly for money—resistance sharpens things. Some shy from putting prose out there because it's a giveaway. You can't fake it. It reveals quality of mind, for better or worse, in a culture where poems can be faked. Find a faker and ask him or her to write anything more substantial than a jacket blurb, and the jig is up.

⌣

Dream life and those sustained times when we have no feeling of ourselves as contingent beings, when the body, *soma*, makes provisional deals with *psyche* and mysteriously finds a way, which *I* still can't yet see, of metabolizing despair, self-hatred, and cowardly despondency.

⌣

When I was getting rid of my books I decided not what to sell or give away but what to keep. I was reviewing my formations, reviewing times when my meetings and greetings were so porous and absorptive. I picked through my books about Greek antiquity, the cults and myths and poems. In my late twenties I wanted to know everything about that remote culture. It wasn't a scholarly interest. I needed to understand what untranslatable values and assumptions saturated the Homeric poems and the tragedies. So much going on at once: the three volumes of Jaeger's *Paideia*, Jane Harrison's *Prolegomena to the Study of Greek Religion*, Walter Otto's great *Dionysus*, Rachel Bespaloff's and Weil's essays on Homer—these were my companions while I was reading ferocious Nietzsche and Pound, all of it going on at once, in a delirious, undirected, self-driven way. My formations were maddened amalgams given the appearance of form by books.

⌇

Poetry shouldn't act needy, or have designs on us or expect our admiration, coddling, etc. It doesn't need neediness if it's doing its work of naming the things of the world, in their orders and messes, and our relations to them. And not only the things of the actual world. It can be a verbal *axis mundi* that connects, through our middle world, the root-knotty, fungal underworld of elementals to the everything-is-nothing supernaturals.

⌇

Certain sounds create a wrap of apparent silence. Windows creaking, wind squeaking through cracks somewhere, the back-and-forth thrashing of treetops that seems so much like *No No No* that I'm convinced I'm hearing them say something with their marvelous silence.

⌇

From the air New York's skyline looks jerry-built, improvised, as much draped raggedly from the atmospheres as it is built *up*. I always expect to see rope bridges impulsively thrown across the nearly perfectly callipered gaps across streets. Chicago's looks modeled, fashioned, carved, as if a hand has just finished its work and gone home—it looks like an artisanal studio or shop. San Francisco's is confectionary, with fanciful and frivolous irregularities, spires, angularities, and pitches lifting and dropping structures as if the ground had been bunched like a rug and left that way. All three cities are money stacked different ways.

François Louis, inventor of the aulochrome, a double soprano sax: "Sound is always the vehicle of emotion, your inside is there in your sound." And Mingus said finding your sound involves imitating somebody else's then being able to conjure up the entire history of the instrument.

~

You want a truly fresh expressiveness, a musicality that's also rich with statement. You want to get life in language, get its sensations flooding the instant of the voiced phrased. But is that even possible? More and more it's as if a veil or smudged glass separates you from whatever is *there*, the life that is in life. And the veil is made of words. It's the words themselves that obstruct you from finding the poetry. If the membrane is made of words, break through words!

~

Women and couples in Klimt's erotic drawings swim in their own sexuality and at the same time swim away from themselves in line and contour. They unveil their sensuousness. Schiele's erotic figures don't unveil, they expose themselves, angular and strung out like guilty things caught. Certain poems unveil themselves with an almost ceremonial patterning, while others are spiky and nervous, as if words were rudely taken hostage to feeling.

~

Bologna, my first visit in several years. In this medieval city, where in the historical center only storefronts change—a women's boutique becomes a high-end candy shop, a shoe store a toy emporium—the past doesn't haunt the present, the present haunts itself. The familiar stucco walls in smoky umbers, leafy reds, scorched yellows, the confined sensation of living in a round walled city. . . . The sensational remembrance of this rushes the present while it *is* all still present. My 2007 *is* my 1972 *and* my 1985.

Poets who are absolutists of the imagination inquire intensely into the world's appearances. Aspiration engorges the nerve ends of their chosen medium. They seek what's sayable, what world images are conceivable and renderable. Nothing aulic or oracular, though, nothing self-admiring or pitched to the world.

⌣

We've been for so long a sick-at-soul country which, like a child trying to convince adults by shouting the same phrase over and over, boasts our spiritual good health, our moral hygiene. How scrupulous we are, especially around election time, about our "moral state." We're self-serving, hypocritical, conflicted, and tirelessly self-celebratory. (God *damn* Whitman.)

⌣

If poets are artists, really, authenticity and artifice are a single act of the imagination.

⌣

Smallish bridge cities like Portland and Pittsburgh offer a string of promises (or tantalizings)—all those visible other sides.

⌣

What can that critic mean who says I am "descriptive not redemptive?" What's the difference? Deliverance? Should poetry deliver us from physical reality? Not if spirit, the non-material vivaciousness of existence, *is* physical reality.

⌣

Empty heart = empty head.

Practice makes perfect. Revision is a poet's practice, as musicians practice hours a day, reiterating sounds of those who have come before and been internalized, while also testing unknown chord changes, tempi, combinations, etc., while playing (as a child plays in a sandbox) over and over the sound one knows. Practice makes imperfect.

⌣

From my broken 1963 paperback of *Portrait of the Artist*, Daedalus pronouncing Aquinas: "*Ad pulcritudinem tria requiruntur integritas, consonantia, claritas.*" "Three things are needed for beauty: wholeness, harmony, and radiance." Here's the update: "Fragmentation, dissonance, darkness." Those get welded to the others. Consequence: completed mixed feeling, chromatic coherence, mysterious aura.

⌣

Freddie Hubbard died. Writers can unawares internalize a musician's sound and model their own on it, that other sonority. Freddie's fat, probing emotional range, his throaty melancholy, could mercilessly elide pity to sweetness to oh-well-fuck-it-ness.

⌣

Memo to literary high society, to the American Academy of Arts and Letters, the American Academy of Arts and Sciences, the Academy of American Poets, the Percy Dovetonsils Poetry Institute, the Mickey Rourke Poetry Society, et alia: Ruskin says in *The Stones of Venice* that an artist "should be fit for the best society, and *should keep out of it.*"

⌣

"It is a curious thing, do you know," Cranly said dispassionately, "how your mind is supersaturated with the religion in which you say you disbelieve."

If self-importance becomes systemic in poetry, nobody notices it anymore. I mean, self-importance not as lyric self-absorption but as preening, but modest, always modest, rectitude, of thought or of sensibility. Poetry should strive to fail on the side of *wrongness*.

⌣

Some festival nights—Halloween, New Year's Eve, the Fourth—I go out late and float neighborhoods, walking and hopping public transit, with stops in bars. (Riding transit is a kind of wheeled walking.) When I float I don't feel I'm passing through time but that it's passing through me, leaving behind its candy wrappers, lost shoes, cooking stains, burnt-rubber atmospheres, and muggy lights. It's a run-on narrative composed of extremely long paragraphs, anecdotes mix-mastered into one strange mossy elixir, like the scummy, algal, life-elongating antioxidant a doctor friend once imposed on me but which, next day, made me sick. Take it anyway, it's good for you.

⌣

The offices of poetry. To use shapely speech to express the radicals of existence in all their ambiguity. To answer idiosyncratically, privately, to a public world given over to falsehood, fake facts, scuzzy rumor, casual murderousness, comedic denials, manic vicious wind tunnel ideologies. To answer palsied language with vital language, plasticity, gaiety of invention and fabulation, over against opportunistic mendacity. If poetry can't, or chooses not to, reveal what it feels like to live as a sentient being in a perilous enchanted world, then maybe it really is marginal or beside the point.

⌣

This terrifying silence of recognizing—it occurs in an instant—the irrelevance of everything: it imposes silence on us and squats, comic-ugly, in the untended garden. It shouldn't be such a task to live in the present conscious of futureness.

26

~

Morning consciousness = a butterfly in flames

~

It's hard to resist glancing at our window reflections. We check for imperfections. We evaluate the project of self-fashioning. "Where doors and walls are made of mirrors," Walter Benjamin says in *The Arcades Project*, "there is no telling outside from in, with all the equivocal illumination." Benjamin never visited New York or San Francisco; he couldn't now say, "women [in Paris] look at themselves more than elsewhere. Before any man catches sight of her, she already sees herself ten times reflected." I get teased that I'll see any French movie set in Paris just to watch the glassfronts. Who cares about the plot of *Un coeur en hiver* or *Nelly et Monsieur Arnaud?* I watch them to swoon over the louvered flash and revolutions of images in restaurant windows, doors, shop windows. Glassfronts make a city whole by fragmenting it. The anarchic multiplicities thrill me.

~

What's wrong with a little *terribilità* now and again? Poetry says, or should say (though not all the time, please) things readers prefer not to hear spoken. It keeps us alert. Poets as spoilers, not pacifiers, saying things unfit for polite company.

~

Three days of silence in my small apartment. It doesn't feel like isolation. The silence feels like a space. Welcome to the monastery. Only chanting allowed. To fill the silence I'm re-reading *Tristes Tropiques*, always restorative, a model of daring, self-correction, making sense of the inner life and the consciousness of the First Ones, those who lived *in illo tempore*, or our imagination of those who lived in the beginnings. To keep poetry, in the day-to-day writing, close to remotest origins and to the instant we're living through.

It's Friday the 13th and the bluebird of happiness alights. (It just arrives, you can't call or catch it.) A scene in *The Pope of Greenwich Village*, Mickey Rourke playing stickball on a lot with his cronies, dressed to kill—shades, white on black loafers, suit and tie. He snaps his fingers and rocks side to side to Sinatra's *Summer Wind*. The perfect moment, the visitation, and suddenly all's right. (Who knew?)

Poetry is a condition, a quality or quiddity of experience—Ali's style as "poetry in motion"; the poetry of a dingy Atlantic City beach; wind beating through trees; Mickey Rourke snapping his fingers— but the poetry that's a human product made in lines and sentences presents as argument, beseeching, moans, invocations, gossip, street obscenities. . . . The writing creates misrule. Days and nights become conjecture in consciousness. You want to compound anything— valium, vicodin, vodka—to slow or narcotize the unconscious, to provide relief from the visually haranguing phantasmagoria that is the wraparound world of the dream life. One night this week I slept three hours then woke to that other poetry: full moon platinum-yellow in my window, the window frame shadows carving up my kitchen floor. Another evening, during a run of rain-hammered days, at sunset a glacial cloud looked pushed up by the horizon line. Albert Pinkham Ryder, Prospero, Odysseus waking on Nausicaa's beach—these and the sunset and the platinum moon become one unwinding pulsing line of my feeling for existence, its time signature.

Yesterday, Friday the 13th, the grocer noticed my tab, $7.77. "That'll bring you good luck!" The calendar as a game of chance. Now, a day later, no good from numbers, no bad from the 13th, and earlier this week there was a gorgeous full moon. No wonder one's mood escalates and drops, jacked-up or dark & fiery & near dead.

You don't realize how driven you've been until one day your fire is just warm coals on a cold morning.

⌣

Does poetry follow the shape of the times, the energies and valuations? Pound's *Cantos* is knowledge heavy. Too heavy. Our own information-driven culture is companioned by a poetry that's information heavy, and data isn't knowledge, which is driven by imagination, not by archival busyness. People talk about poems as if they were cleverly designed, efficient data centers or delivery systems. The musical and the mythy may be effectively gone for good.

⌣

It's March and the light lasts longer. Ashy clouds coming into a perfect horseshoe but now amassing to resemble a boar that changes to a croc's tail. Come, go, dissolve, transform. Ovid, Tu Fu, Constable. The clouds mock the stability, solidity, and pacific stillness of houses deployed below, their lighted windows mirroring skylights, chimneys, and a shade of blue light stopped in one bay window far east. That's my window I'm seeing from my window. Another place, my place, in mind. The barely discernible stranger behind the window looking out on all this, from that far window, is me. Condensations of illusion in memory's neural factories. And way out there, above the Marin bluffs, lacustrine mountains and salt lakes, dragging with them their own gossipy gang of clouds.

⌣

St. Catherine of Siena: "The Absolute Innocence of all within my creation/takes a while to understand." (What innocence?)

⌣

Ongoing transformations, multiple manifestations, gods and goddesses with many arms and avatars who themselves change into yet other avatars. Hindu consciousness, as it flows through the major texts, is fluid, labile, horrendously violent. Many rivers with infinite tributaries and branches. In *Ka* Roberto Calasso describes the figure of Prajāpati—Lord of the Creatures, Progenitor, antecedent of Brahmâ. "Prajāpati was mind as power to transform. And to transform itself. Nothing else can so precisely be described as overflowing, boundless, inexpressible." All's change. Change itself is a changing entity, assuming different processes, mechanics, evidence. Readers maddened by Whitman are maddened by his Hindoo self-ness. One state changes to another without explanation. He's himself, Walt, one of the roughs, among us, yet also among the dead who lie beneath the leaves of grass, whose hair is those leaves, and Walt's there, too, in the leaves a-growing. Look for him on a ferry, eyeing a young bargeman, and under the soles of your feet. Now you see him, now you don't.

⌒

To write a poem that isn't just a sustained concentrate of feeling but *about* that condition, that effort to live intensely, write intensely, and maybe not even know the difference.

⌒

Craving a simplicity and plainness of mind I've never known. To break the circuit of how I perceive and live out my perception of the things of the world (and my work and me). A conversation with my Buddhist friend S., who reminds me that no such circuit really exists, neither does the reality that generates it. All's illusion, Herr Filosof. But how arrive at that condition of mind, that mentality? Me? A William James flesh-and-nerve-ends poet? An unreality, but maybe the only way to live in the world and not be hostage to its contingencies and mechanics. How do I begin in world fatigue and work to conceive and think outside delusional, self-enhancing habits of thought?

⌒

You told me the Incan Trinity ironwork—the eagle on the back of a jaguar that stands on a snake (it's an oxidized chalky green now)—means spirit on strength on smarts. How feeble those abstractions sound considering the natural history of the originals. Though the figures themselves are unfinished, barely articulated, nearly abstract forms of the animals they represent. And that thought measures the distance between me and wilderness, between me and lived shared sacred story. So I do the modern thing and make of this Trinity (I know much about the other one) a companion amulet, an object of secular devotion, and keep it with my single-candle household shrine that remembers nothing and everything. It sustains me in my own wants and desires. Kneeling there, I feel like a believing fool. Trinity and its candle will keep me alert to existence while I empty the mind except for the action of the fire and ask no question about what might be beyond consciousness.

⌣

Writing about loss thrills and energizes because loss is another form of transformation—that's its grievous, dismal, fiery promise.

⌣

To wake at night to rainfall is as closed off and reserved an experience as monastic chant. Tonight the pitting and tip-tap business is now a whipping and flapping, the gods throwing down rain as if it were hateful debris dumped on us for some as yet unannounced malfeasance, mortals offending gods, which we were born to do.

⌣

Poets aren't aware of their astonishment in the presence of reality until they've written out the astonishment.

⌣

I go for long passages when the involuntary circulatory action of existence, the mechanics of it, run down and feel about to stop. That's when the clichés run me down: Time Is Running Out. The Clock, She Is Ticking. Make Hay While the Shoe Shines. An obtuse reviewer says (of me) that poets traditionally get the blues, so what's the big deal? The blues is the blues. Yes, indeed. And it's a drifty weariness, a slowing of wanting to make the effort of wanting to stay alive, stay in motion. . . . How extravagant! To make my residence close to the membrane between here and *there*, somethingness and nothingness. Oh, such ease and comfort in despair. That becomes the short-roll player piano tune that loops in consciousness. Try to escape it. I dare you.

Cue oboes and bassoons!

Hecklers, cue kazoos!

⁓

In Tintoretto's *Baptism of Christ*, light radiates down from the dove of the Holy Spirit like flakey coins that turn to water in the dish St. John holds. Light materializes as life-sustaining water. Light and water wash down the picture and over Christ's head and around his body—it's the yonder made earthly, spirit transformed to sensuality, Christ composed of water an emanation-condensation of the light of the Trinity.

⁓

The tender, liquid beauty of clothes drying on a line, the wind blowing through them.

And the beauty of those who *live* the garments, who fill them, so bonded to their own absence.

⁓

Easter was the only feast day (though there wasn't much feasting involved) that mattered to me as a boy. I didn't know then, but it's because it was Resurrection Time. Initiation, ritualized annually, the Christian version of recurring rebirth, restoration of the puny self to the universe and the deity that the universe is. As I got older, that jump of unreason to belief and faith—trapeze artistry, was it? some kind of derangement? Shestov says it's absolutely an act of unrea-son—was hammered so constantly by the stolid stubborn adherence to the irrational in my culture that I began to need things to answer to reason, deliberation, *sense*. That eventually kills one's feeling for the sacred in daily life. Easter still matters, but as a recurrent energy of emergence detached completely from the thought or imaging in mind of Jesus' intervention in history. That's shriveled and puny. It needs to be more than cultural opportunism, or random colonizing by a depleted and desiccated and barren Western consciousness. The New Jerusalem is Mind; it's the still mysterious operations of the brain.

⌒

To hold the sensation of the ongoingness of experience in a structure, to make a poem the mechanics of pulling it into a structure, or what *feels* like a structure, with sensation and thinking morphing, gyrating, backtracking—to invent and in the same instant absorb experience. How can poetry possibly keep up? How represent a fluidity of recognition that carries a tragic sense of existence, tragedy as an action embedded in the fevered action of the words?

⌒

Summer solstice now passed, finally. Certain days during homely sorrowing panics, the dialing of the sun and arcing of the moon bring a grief hardly bearable (but bear it we do), and with grief, promise, until there's a confounding and one *is* the other. We inhabit both spiritual cosmic conditions, sorrow and hope, in the same baffling moment, same season, same exhalation of soul-life.

⌒

In my Hart Crane dream he's dressed like a dashing 1950s movie star—wool suit, necktie, white shirt. Hovering in the air of the dream, not a voice quite, but a meaning somehow voiced by the dream atmosphere: "Get the sound right, don't worry about obscurity, don't worry about being understood."

⌒

Habit is a stabilizing psycho-biological compass. I take a walk as soon as I get home after even a short flight, not just because I don't have a car and the ground is where I feel ready to deal with the things of the world, but because when I'm up in the ether I feel physically incomplete. Locomotion makes me more palpable to myself, fleshed out, self-locatable.

―⌣―

I'm listening to Roy Hargrove's "Starmaker" track. He gets such a cavernous, throaty voice from the flugelhorn. It's as if the song wants us, desires us. Music is a medium for desire that sets, tracks, addresses our moods, but the notion that desire actually originates in the music mystifies me. "Starmaker," over and over, same track, same performance, surprise and fibrillating intimacy every time, the heart going through its changes, and the heart is full of yearning. It's not that I'm hearing it as if for the first time, but I *am* hearing it anew, and I carry into the repeat a memory of past experience composed of an identical set of musical facts. The repeat, the return or replay, makes for a circular coming-into-consciousness that may be the closest I'll ever come to a vision of round time. I don't understand the process, but it has to do with a quality of music and any art that's memorable. It reawakens us to the intensities of existence, and it's saying, "I want you." That's what freshness is.

―⌣―

American eloquence, our anti-eloquence, our vernacular, on the streets and in the fields.
Item: A Mexican migrant laborer picking lettuce in Texas, when asked if he owned any land: "I don't even own the dirt under my fingernails."
Item: Next to me at my corner bus stop, a broken-down guy wearing headphones:
"Hey, man, this bus go all the way to the Marina?"
—*All the way to the other side of town.*
"These busses, goddamn, go all over the place!"
—*They do that.*
"But there should be a subway takes you from one end of town to another."
—*I grew up in a subway city; I like subways.*

"Yeah, let me tell you, those subways are really something, I mean in big cities like New York and New Jersey."

⌒

Calvino, writing about lightness in *Six Memos for the Next Millennium*: "It's the sudden, agile leap of the poet-philosopher who raises himself above the weight of the world, showing that with all his gravity he has the spirit of lightness." Freshness isn't a quality, like lightness, or an action, like surprise. A maker can craft lightness or surprise. If we make art we can hope for freshness but not shape or instill it: if we think we can, we're contriving and conniving, and the work will turn mechanical and stamp itself with an expiration date. In his prison cell, Richard II reflects with ineffectual grandeur on the frustration of creating it with metaphor making: "I have been studying how I may compare / This prison where I live unto the world; / And for because the world is populous / And here is not a creature but myself, / I cannot do it." He tries anyway but is condemned to a staleness unto death. Freshness is an aura or perfume. It's a condition, a state where we're unaware preservation is or has been even taking place. And it can only be possessed by things we've experienced, frequently, for a long time. Something provokes astonishment the first time we know it, then ten months or ten years later it does the same, and we don't even remember the first astonishment. Freshness is a faint narcissism that the work itself possesses.

⌒

Imitation and Signature. A loose sheet falls from an old notebook. On it, in the handwriting of my early twenties, is Donne's "His Parting from Her."

> Since she must go and I must mourn, come night,
> Environ me with darkness, whilst I write;
> Shadow that hell unto me, which alone
> I am to suffer when my love is gone.

Under those lines I'd written my own carry-on:

Sleep whatever night can sleep with me,
She's off to where there's waking and light.
No light breaks or interferes with grief
In this steep climb of words . . .

How memory markers, time's traces, change! To date a piece of a life, a zone of experience where one was in the primitive stages of proofing aspirations. To date things by how the handwriting looks! The changing handwriting in the notebooks over many years—shrinking, crimping, wrinkling, inflating, getting straighter or crookeder—is an autobiographical emblem.

⌒

After a reading & talk at the Studio School, my audience mostly artists and "art people," a student says how unusual it is for a poet to write so intimately about art, and a much older artist responds (excitably) on my behalf: "Baudelaire! Baudelaire! Don't you know?" Who does know? In conversations about poetry and visual art, I don't hear much talk, adversarial or otherwise, about that value so central to those conversations one hundred years ago—the tradition, at least as Eliot and Pound and Moore and Williams assumed it to be. Now tradition is a rowdier company, it includes the traditions of traditional societies. (Brodsky once chastised a young Hispanic poet I knew for including Spanish in a poem in English, denouncing the inclusion of non-English speech in an English language poem. How modern is that?) The visual artists long ago breached the confines—Picasso and Matisse and African tribal costuming, Brancusi and ancient Romanian carvers, Giacometti and those Cycladic fetish-makers. Baudelaire! Baudelaire!

⌒

The oldest church in the contiguous complex of Bologna's Santo Stefano, believed to be built on a cult site dedicated to Isis, *looks* pagan. It's round. Christianity absorbed the spherical, the form of eternal recurrence, and boxed it up within the rectangle, a squared off, gabled or peaked space, as if to restrain that energy. That early Church chamber is adjacent to a tenth century church, a bare cold place with a squat primitive stone altar, the foundations of the *chiesa spettacolare* of Renaissance popes. Here, as in Isis' temple, images seem unnecessary: these are spaces where conversations and voiced prayer would occur during the celebration of the sacrament. And this altar reminds us that faith's central celebration is sacrifice.

⌒

My editor writes she can't publish my new book because Random House is being "restructured" and the German parent company won't let her contract books with "negative profit-loss projections."

⌒

The lyric. It's not the nature of the self that matters, not the gigantism of subjectivity wherein lies the Power, but in experience unveiled. The lyric's formal action is the drawing back of the veils, the shape of the disclosure of feeling. Our culture is addled with a rapture for personalities, originals, salient presences: experience is subservient to "voice," viz. personality—pious, politically aligned, "human" beyond the proper and modest confines of humanness. It shouldn't be the "me" that matters but the kind of music the me can make of the rawness of its experience.

⌒

Kierkegaard: "The whole of existence frightens me."

From the 1990s

"What is hardest to confess is not what is criminal, but what is ridiculous and shameful."—Rousseau's *Confessions*

~

I write to express a state of nerves deliberative and self-aware, an intensity of the moral moment. I'm put off by intellectual confections. Temperament can determine the rhythms and textures of any poet's language. Choleric and melancholic, I expect my work to be dyed with those colors. I lack patience and sedate expansiveness yet am drawn to poets who create capacious symphonic effects—Wordsworth of *The Ruined Cottage* and *The Prelude*—where life and moral consequence open in a broad physical context. Wordsworth couldn't achieve what his sometime friend Coleridge did: he couldn't turn rudeness or clatter or splinteriness or fragmentariness into a virtue. Coleridge's poems, even *Christabel* and the *Rime*, are racy sketches. Diderot says that sketches represent a fevered love and energy on the artist's part "with no admixture of the affected elaboration introduced by thought: through the sketch the artist's very soul is poured forth on the canvas."

~

The checkout clerks in my local suburban supermarket speak Spanish and English. Sometimes a cashier chatting in English with a customer glances back at me and switches to Spanish. I look at the women and men, mostly working people in manual or secretarial jobs, many with kids, and in the kids I see future poets, from a culture that contains and protects them in the envelop of its own language and customs, though there's also violence and all sorts of discontent and trouble. Some of these kids may write poetry in an English saturated with the manners and feeling tones of their native language and maybe cauled by a memory of a distant place. It will be pure mongrel American. Their poetry will remember the work of today's Latino poets with an arrogance and impatience poets have to exercise, they may respect their predecessors for clearing a way but criticize them for relying on local color, cultural anecdotalism, and bully politics. At home in their languages, they drag along behind their parents' shopping carts in the big Lucky's supermarket in this bland suburban setting. Bland except for the storefront produce stand one block down that reminds me so piercingly of the festive colors of open air markets in Italian cities. "El Mercadito Latino," its bins overflowing with cobbled textures of limes, avocadoes, oranges, bananas, lemons, apples. The poets are there, buying plantains and tomatillos with their mothers. When the clerk finishes talking with the others in Spanish, she looks at me and asks: "Is that all for today, sir?"

⌒

Rereading myself. One darkly marbled seam down the years is some kind of American-style *canzoniere*, the story of one love, one marriage, compounded of all other loves. Lyric trouble and pain between the one who desires and the one desired. Damage, desperate affection, betrayals, acidic reproaches, sometimes all these mashed together. The canzoniere's energy spots—the Bay Area, South Louisiana, Chicago: fogland, bayou, snowscape—the scenic *is* the narrative, its scenes are an imaging of eros. How can it be that the actual wife, the woman who is the current down all those years, when she read my *Selected Poems*, wanted to know why she hardly appears. She can't see herself there. Yet I see her everywhere in the poems. How failed an aspiration is that?

⌒

Yesterday I was walking down Via San Vitale in Bologna, having just come from Via San Leonardo, the working-class quarter where the colors of housefronts wane through reds and yellows and oranges, a synoptic seasonality on the plaster, while along the portico people walked briskly, shopped at the unmarked produce stand that just last week was a garage, or swept the pavements. But I ended up on Via San Vitale, one of the main streets that spoke toward the center of town where the two towers stand: Asinelli, tall and complete despite the earthquakes that rattled it in earlier times; Garisenda, Dante's tower, which in his poem gives scale and vertiginous pitch to the figure of the giant Antaeus, leaning over the Pilgrim on hell's floor. Before coming to the towers, I passed my favorite palazzo, *il Fantuzzi*, called *Il palazzo degli elefanti* because of the ornamental carvings of elephants on the facade, a funny and extravagantly oriental decoration on these medieval streets. The years have eroded the stonework. The elephants' high relief has been planed nearly flat, bleared: they look like yesterday's sand castles. The sunlight, slanting through the portico pillars, rules the shadows into even parts. The sun dials across the pavements. Smoke, fumes, odors from houses, cigarettes, coffee machines, perfumes and colognes, cheese and salami, and vehicles of all sorts running along the narrow street. A lady pedals by on an old bicycle that seems made of wrought iron; she's wearing a mink coat and kid gloves—I can see the beautiful balled shape of knucklebones and wrist. I tell myself: this is my place. But it's not my place. I feel like I've always been here and never really so, because I always feel like a visitor wherever I am. While walking down Via San Vitale I was where I *really* am, right now, in Redwood City, California, where there are no redwoods, where there are few tall trees of any kind. Redwood City is famous for having the most moderate weather west of the Rockies; the town's official motto used to be "Climate Best, by Government Test." The elephants look down on me as I say it, shedding their outlines.

⌒

Strange that there's so little interesting poetry of religious belief, especially since world events more and more are driven by belief (or the fanaticism of Eastern or Western Fundamentalisms). Somebody asks me what I believe. I believe in the suspicion of transcendence,

43

in the capacity of consciousness to imagine a transcendent order as an objective reality. I believe in my own unbelief.

⌣

If you live with whatever you call depression—melancholia, the black dog, the noontide demon—you smell it in other poets like a rotten-petals perfume. William Cowper in a 1790 letter: "I number the nights as they pass, and in the morning bless myself that another night is gone, and no harm has happened." You live in terror of the momentous ordinary. Awareness of your vulnerability doesn't help. "We are not always wiser for our knowledge, and I can no more avail myself of mine, than if it were in the head of another man, and not in my own." We know what the worst passages of the year will be. For Cowper it cycled in January: "I now see a long winter before me. I know the ground before I tread upon it; it is hollow, it is agitated, it suffers shocks in every direction." For me it's April, a paralysis induced by flowerings and restorations; new green and growing things agonize and terrify me. The heart can't stand so much blessedness and bestowals; the hatefulness and fear burn inward like a spooling flame. The unremittingness is as rude and tedious as what I'm now writing.

⌣

Intellectual nostalgia, I thought, rereading Camus. Some feebleness in the need to recover (if it's even possible) the austerity and force of his books that I felt twenty-five years ago:

> To understand is, above all, to unify. The mind's deepest desire, even in its most elaborate operations, parallels man's unconscious feeling in the face of his universe: it is an insistence upon familiarity, an appetite for clarity. . . . That nostalgia for unity, that appetite for the absolute illustrates the essential impulse of the human drama.

I think form in poetry is an expression of that nostalgia, but the absolute isn't what I want, I want the appetite, the plasticity of that. It's not a wish for perfection. Poetry's formal energies are appetitive because they insist, often in a disorderly way, on the acquisition of all the particulars of experience, of an impossible sum and constellation of instances. The forms of poetry may be a judicious processional or dizzy dance, but they are nearly always a masque enacting nostalgia for the absolute. The incompleteness and incompletability of that activity, of the exercise of that appetite, is one kind of story a poet might tell.

⌣

A photo by Roman Vishniac of Jews in the Warsaw Ghetto. Falling snow, men standing outdoors dressed in shabby, ill-fitting overcoats, shoes too large (the toes curl as if recoiling from the cold ground), long white and dark beards set off against the black buildings and bright snow. The mothy snow falls and stops, suspended leafily in the air of the picture, soft but obliterating because there seem to be too many snowflakes falling, with no sign of warmth or shelter anywhere. It's an image of exposure and reduction. Not diminution, for the figures look dominant and occupy so much space, thanks to those huge coats. The enclosures, the buildings, awnings, shawls, shoes, even the snow cowling the entire scene— every bit is expressive of exposure. The figures don't exist in or with the elements, they *suffer* them. Heavily wrapped, they're yet bare fork'd creatures.

⌣

The poet, unawares, quivers with awareness of the past, the actual, and the always, experienced as one moment of the soul.

⌣

Paradise is where objects have a hard bright singleness not numbed or clouded by habit, by what Baudelaire calls "the heavy darkness of communal and day-to-day existence." The more habituated we become, while objects proliferate so riotously in the culture around us, the harder it is to keep the sensors alive and keen, to preserve our

Eden sense. Maybe we're so flooded by objects of habit that we live in a nearly constant state of distraction from the shining particulars of existence that strike us on every page of Homer, and we tend to seek meanings, privileged meanings, in whatever is idiosyncratic and strange. We insist more and more on certain moments, picked from the bin of identical parts, as unique, freighted with meaning or consequence. The poet in a secular time still nostalgic for the absolute (but unwilling or unable to engage that discipline) will confer on the entirely subjective moment the singular brilliance of Paradise. We live with a sense of bereavement, and of it we make a poetry that knows but is reluctant to admit that the world outside consciousness is made up simply of this, that, and the other thing. If Eden is what we want it to be, it is not Eden.

⌒

The first early winter rain, after three years of drought, comes just before dawn. I thought I heard the falling drops inside my head, felt them somehow even before I heard them, little sleepy drumrolls, then came the tangy charred odor that finally woke me.

Rain now off and on for two days. Too soon, they say. (After drought years!) Vintners worry about the harvest. The grapes, especially the delicate whites, need a long dry season. Yet the rain feels restorative, an indifferent pounding plenitude.

⌒

We find our own speed. Somebody says I walk fast and I wonder what counts for fastness of foot compared to the twenty-mile jaunts of a Wordsworth or Keats or Coleridge. And their pace wasn't up to Audubon's. When he describes in his journals and letters the distances he covered in a day, it's clear the man wasn't walking really, he was springing forward in a walking kind of way. The velocity of a stride can measure a person's pace through the mined gardens of circumstance, through work and loves and changing emotional frequencies. Two persons walking together at speed, telling stories and breathing hard, will physically draw closer, hands in pockets, bump shoulders, and the bump might incite something unexpected and intense, or not.

～

A well-behaved poetry, self-assured and anxious not to displease, makes politeness into a suave arrogance. Good manners become a way of coercing readers into admiration. Coerced, they think they're being charmed. This is our Alexandrianism, maybe appropriate to the end of our century, but it's *politically* dangerous.

～

A tradition in Abruzzo, where my father was born, was to take a newborn after it has been washed and wrapped, and set it down on the earth so that it touches its first mother and its soul is "grounded." I like to think my father was thus grounded, though I have no proof he was. Born here instead of "over there," I should have been made to touch the ground. It might have helped me mineralize the vapors of imagination.

～

Clinical melancholia doesn't color one's feeling for reality, it determines it. The fall of light, a child's laughter, a lover's whisper, wind unsettling curtains, a towhee hopping on grass—every moment is fraught with fatefulness. The most delicate things become fatty deposits of the worst-is-yet-to-come. Flight, the sight of it, induces the agony of impossibility—a gull oaring itself into the air makes you weep because it's a grandiose vision of the impossible. Gravity rules. It defines you, and you are null. The bed is the best and worst place. It's the island where you're safe, if not from the serrated confabulations of your own consciousness, at least from afflictions the world beyond the bed will, you're certain, bring you. It's the worst place because the longer you're there, the more it loves you, the more it renews its sticky torpor. It's a safe place to consider killing yourself.

Coleridge, mad dog of discriminations and divisiveness, *suffered* the differences among things. "Sea, hill, and wood, / This populous village! Sea, and hill, and wood." He suffered most the abyss separating nature from consciousness. Wordsworth is the surveyor of things come together in mutual blessing. He views consciousness, he doesn't suffer it. He's quick to admit strangers to his banquet. Coleridge must first question any stranger about his origins and destination and means of travel. Then he goes back to the kitchen to revise the evening's menu.

Eliade says that poets try to remake the world, to see it as if neither time nor history exists, and that this attitude is like that of the "primitive," of the person in traditional society. We don't live in a traditional society. Most poets coming out of a European tradition, certainly those in North America, write out of the ruins or remnants or inchoate beginnings of different traditions, dozens of traditions, religious, mythological, familial, political. I know that a poet seeks and, when fortunate, succeeds in seeing (to use Eliade's phrase) *in illo tempore*, in the First Time, the Early Time, in or near Paradise, which means "walled garden." But poets write of and with the body, which is pure contingency, time, and an image of history. I may desire to remake or re-see the world in its First Time, as it was in the beginning, but I know in that moment of desire that it's a picture of impossibility, that I write out of the contingency of body, hour, event. If the "pure" or "primitive" poet seeks to remake the world, he or she does so in the shadow of Nimrod, master builder of the Tower of Babel.

In *The Varieties of Religious Experience*, William James says that the life of religion consists of the belief that "there is an unseen order, and that our supreme good lies in harmoniously adjusting ourselves thereto." But much poetry comes from the process of failing to so adjust, or of the torment and struggle to adjust, the dissonance and raucousness of the work of it. I think a poet's work is to tell the struggle, to attempt to reveal the order or our dream of it. Poetry that convincingly and freshly declares knowledge of that harmony or makes sweet music of that agreement is rare. Traherne and Vaughan do it. Such poetry may be a little superfluous, for who needs to have represented what has been so supremely experienced? To satisfy religious desire, Hopkins turned language itself into a kind of gigantomachy.

I was attracted to church decoration when I was young not just because my house was austere and drab but because vessels, statuary, stained glass, and wall reliefs physically thrilled me. The sacred narrative represented in the Stations of the Cross that marked a Way up and down church aisles melted to a plain, satisfying sensuousness of forms. The marble reliefs were sexy. The pumiced curves of bicep and buttock, the turned foot or muscled thigh, were stunning emergencies of flesh. I liked to imagine reaching my hand out to stroke the tense forearm of a centurion or one of the women crowding around Christ as he climbs to Golgotha. They reminded me of the pale muscular flesh of my parents and relatives that I was allowed to see uncovered only during short summer vacations at the South Jersey shore. The stained glass images were very different, not at all familial or fleshly. They gleamed by virtue of light originating outside, drenched with a holiness that seemed almost alien to the church itself. More than those voluptuous wall reliefs, the figures of disciples and saints in the stained glass, the images of lamb, bull, eagle, dove, begged for a response and determined the kind of response. They predetermined desire and drained it of its charge, its fever. The Stations' remoteness, their material self-containment, made desire looser and wilder, more fanciful even. My feelings could play in the space between the stone and my self. During Good Friday ceremony, a large crucifix was set down by the altar rail—I remember the corpus being about my size, I was ten years old—and like other devotees I approached the image on my knees and kissed its feet. In that moment all my feelings for the anxiety, the suffering and death, the promise of resurrection and restoration to a life elsewhere—those feelings froze in me, I wasn't willing to surrender them to an image of Christ that was so grabbily realistic and literal. That small distance of desire, between me and the images of the Stations, was crucial to my belief. I needed that space to work in.

⌒

A pure American tone? The yellow of the vinyl kitchen stool James Stewart's Scottie climbs in *Vertigo* to test his acrophobia. It's *our* yellow of postwar American prosperity, which Vice-President Richard Nixon bragged about to Nikita Khrushchev. Aggressive cheer, bloated self-confidence, strident belief in work and getting ahead. *Vertigo*'s yellow is blazon for those values, the same values toyed with, mocked, and exploited to great commercial success by Pop artists of the 1960s, who took over that hopped-up yellow that gleams like chrome but looks saturated with creamy mango pulp. Or the coppery-red wall coverings in Ernie's, the classy old San Francisco room where Scottie first sees the woman he'll lose twice. That red, too, became a Pop favorite, also the red of the Coke sign that pops up somewhere else. The colors aren't tantalizing, they're annunciatory. They don't stir desire; they announce desire's fulfillment, in the signs of material righteousness. It's a joy that wants no suggestion of danger or peril to disturb its perfections, though *Vertigo*'s narrative aches with menace and delusional desire and loss. Having lost the woman he loved, Scottie finds another and crafts her in a perfect image of the one lost, only to discover that she's the irreplaceable original after all. Finding that out, he loses her a second time.

⌒

We brood so much on childhood and adolescence because we know (too late!) how formative and determinant they were. We make of their events and personalities an allegory which, if fully witnessed and understood, will instruct us (we trust) in how we're still being baked in the kiln of present experience. If we really do believe adulthood is process, a time of continued spiritual motion and progress, and not a tyranny of norms, habits, childhood legends, by inquiring into *anything* of our early life we ask permission to go on being in process of becoming. Reflection and recollection thus become one act of prayer.

～

In my twenties I studied Yeats's essays and *Autobiographies* nearly as much as his poetry. It gave me some (perhaps useless) sense of how poetry issues from workaday intellectual activity. In college, it seemed all the poets I read wrote prose of a serious kind— Milton, Dryden, Keats (the letters!), Shelley, Crane (more letters!), Eliot, Moore, Lawrence, Pound, Williams. I became persuaded, unawares, that when poets weren't writing poetry they were writing something else, writing in the world, or translating. Yeats kept the poetry and prose in excited balance, as Keats did with his letters. In both we hear self-instruction and intellectual desire. Keats (like Crane) was exemplary because he conducted his education in public, in the processional developments in the poems chronicled in the letters. Eliot seemed, for all his apparent authority, evasive in a priestly way I recognized from having been educated by priests. Lawrence was a fearless, obnoxious gusher, exciting to me because he was nuttily uncontainable. Of later poets, Tate, Ransom, Schwartz (beautiful rotting Delmore), Lowell and Berryman were all college teachers, as I am, but I had no notion that a poet's place was in a creative writing program and that classroom pontification would become the normalized substitute for a poet's prose practice, that the workshop would become the poet's public.

～

Attention isn't an act of the will; it's an instinct to hold on to what's given.

～

St. Paul, Romans 8:22: "The whole creation groaneth and travaileth in pain together." It's the pain of contingency, and yet we in developed nations take for granted comforts unthinkable one hundred years ago. We live in relative ease without servants. Schools and churches are warm in winter, cool in summer. We have most of our teeth. We're not reminded indoors and out that we live in a world of shit and pus and garbage. Most people at all levels of society wear whole clothing and don't smell bad. Constantly present to us are images of glassy perfection, on TV and in movies, where action and consequence are perfectly timed and human beings practice behavior meant to be watched. What, then, groans and travails and we along with it? The perfections of civilization don't (yet) eliminate death and change. Postponements, concealments, mock transfigurations, and legends of death experiences outside the living body—these we know. We can dull or numb pain, as many indigenous peoples have known how to do for centuries, but we can't eliminate it. The body is a world of hurts, a library or memory bank of change. The passion of our technological imagination, however, more and more abstracts us from our world of pain and natural fact. Control and more control. It's human consciousness, anyway, that formulates the community and solidarity of suffering that Paul describes. The machinery of refinement makes our lives less constantly challenged by contingency. All the more reason to reckon that we are always one beat away from Paul's words.

⌒

Ruskin writes in *Val d'Arno*:

> Writers and painters of the Classic school set down nothing but what is known to be true, and set it down in the perfectest manner possible in their way, and are thenceforward authorities from whom there is no appeal. Romantic writers and painters, on the contrary, express themselves under the impulse of passions which may indeed lead them to the discovery of new truths, or to the more delightful arrangements or presentment of things already known: but their work, however brilliant or lovely, remains imperfect, and without authority.

Most art in the past century has been post-Romantic, driven by the impulse of whatever's uncertain, unstable, brilliantly or garishly imperfect or raw from the world. Yet a lot of recent poetry and painting asserts certainty and knowingness. Now at the end of the twentieth century, we may be more susceptible than ever to fake sophrosyne, more needy of final authorities and formal certainties. We're still looking through pieces of the broken lens of authority. As if to give us a critical precept for moral thinking and feeling in our time, Nietzsche said there were no facts, only perspectives on facts. Poets, more than before, I think, and maybe in response to this, offer personal experience or uniqueness of sensibility as the only authority from which there is no appeal. It's a mongrel version of classical need crossed with Romantic profligacy and solipsism. Ruskin contrived his categories at the end of his century. At the end of ours, we can't trust the contrivance of these or any categories. We want no more types or classes of things, only instances. And yet poets need patterns of instances and will, if necessary, make or contrive such patterns.

━

L=A=N=G=U=A=G=E poets treat poetry as problematic: writing isn't primarily expressive, it's a kind of diagnostic display of problems given to us with the use of language. Wittgenstein is more a covering presence for them than Bergson. What is the pictorial identity of a statement in words? "You cannot say what you cannot say?" These poets are at least confronting issues raised by philosophers of language, issues that sooner or later have consequences for the words of poetry. L=A=N=G=U=A=G=E poetry isn't very satisfying, though, and isn't post-Romantic enough. For all the unintelligibility of the poems—if, that is, we expect poems to give intelligible reports of shared realities—they seem perfect and complete in their problematic nature.

━

William Cowper cannily and amicably conceals his secret suicidal melancholia in the flowering shrubs of his letters, which craft a rather wholesome, amiable personality, but he admits to "[putting] on an air of cheerfulness and vivacity to which I am in reality a stranger." It was "the arduous task of being merry by force. . . . Despair made amusements necessary, and I found poetry the most agreeable amusement." He lived with the unwanted companion and made himself a good one. His pain, his madness, was the raised, rough grain of his sense of failure in belief, in life as devotion. To feel unworthy of God is, in derangement, to be convinced of being unworthy of life.

—

The great collection of French paintings from the Barnes Foundation is broken up and packaged for a touring exhibition, the first time paintings have left the Foundation established by Alfred Barnes several decades ago at his residence in Merion, Pennsylvania. Its first venue in 1993 was the National Gallery in Washington. Only the flashiest items were selected. I was there opening day. The large Tintoretto-esque dancers Matisse painted for the lunettes in the main salon of the Foundation, hung in the denatured culture-space of the museum, looked disoriented and abstracted. The tone of spectators seeing the works for the first time was mostly peevish, resentful that Barnes had "selfishly" kept these masterpieces "all to himself," though for many years anyone willing to reserve a time and make the short trip from Philadelphia could spend hours with the collection. But that proprietary veil of seclusion insulted people's democratic sense of things. Many who made the trip to Merion before the recent renovations were horrified by the ambience, the stuffy rooms, the seedy lighting (one chandelier in the center of the large rooms, the rest natural light). Whenever I visited I saw the works literally in a different light, depending on season, time of day, and weather. Yet the paintings always looked fresh and responsive, their subtleties dimmed or sharpened depending on the illumination. The outraged tone of impatient spectators at the National Gallery suggests that Americans feel they have the *right* to see art treasures amassed by millionaire tycoons (who themselves have every right to acquire those millions in the American way, by any means necessary). Somebody like Barnes, who denied public general access to the aura of those paintings, was un-American and an ungenerous creep. It's grotesque to hear these feelings expressed by Americans who would kill (or file a lawsuit) to protect their rights to private ownership and the exclusivity and entitlements of ownership.

⌁

Philip Larkin's poetry is what his admirers want it (and him) to be. Melancholy but not impolitely or menacingly or tragically so. Worldly but cynical about his own worldliness. Capable of appreciating the appeal of aspiration, especially the desire for transcendence, but sensible enough to know how feckless aspiration is. Endlessly self-critical, impregnably knowing, reluctantly (but endlessly) self-absolving. Not that Larkin's sagging sense of endurable aggrievedness isn't genuine; it's just tame and listless. One subject is Romanticism gone sour—in nature, household, heart. He disliked art (bop, literary modernism, cubism) that overrides boundaries and makes formal invention an expression of appetite or desire. His owlish contrariness is theatrical and controlling. Most good poems have rhetorical energies. Larkin's suggest we're fools (or less than adult) to think about existence differently from the vision the poems give. Line by line, his timing is exquisitely cagey and helps him contrive his cool conversational audacity (we all know what mum and dad do to us, now, don't we?). I'd save "Here," "The Whitsun Weddings," and his best poem, "The Explosion," about a mining disaster, which figures forth life's impermanence in a dream phantom carrying an egg. It bleeds through the amorphous boundaries of form and feeling that the rest of his work stands in modest bittersweet disapproval of.

⌁

World sorrow. There should be a single word in English for that. If we're awake to the fact that human action is a way of serving a dream of existence, we're liable to feel an overpowering helplessness and irrelevance—the irrelevance of everything, a suicidal irrelevance—and its physical expression is cryptic silence and self-removal. It's systemic, a toxin in the circulatory system of spirit. You don't contract it, *it comes for you*, genetically and in the world—it weaves its tacky filaments into your temperament. When in melancholia, the body wakes from dreams feeling like a gummy slab, as if the effort of dreaming depletes the soul's energy to rise.

⌣

Love's redemption isn't answerable to reason, theory, or will. We collapse into it. The way down points the way up. When Raskolnikov, doing hard labor in Siberia for his crime, literally collapses into love, Dostoyevsky describes it thus: "How it happened he himself did not know, but suddenly it was as if something lifted him and flung him down at [Sonya's] feet" (in the great Pevear/Volokhonsky translation). Moments later, they realize that the seven years of Raskolnikov's imprisonment would be both unbearable suffering and infinite happiness, and D. comments: "But he was risen and he knew it." Risen like Lazarus, whose story obsesses R. earlier in the novel. Wrapped wormlike in the cerements of nihilism, of Napoleonic conceits, willfulness, and awful nervous anguish, he's finally freed *without reason* to arise. Falling at Sonya's feet, he's exalted. Both actions become one movement of the Soul and its love.

⌣

Nietzsche and Wittgenstein. They practiced philosophy in a way that makes them models for poets—they systematically and joyfully philosophized against themselves.

⌣

My feeling for inadequacy. Giacometti is the hero of the time, practicing the joy and passion of form-finding while also convinced that everything fails. The work is bound to fall short of what the imagination wants it to become. I've lived so long with these convictions that they begin to feel like a romance or a consoling manner. In *All Things Are Possible* Shestov says: "Creative activity is a continual progression from failure to failure, and the condition of the creator is usually one of uncertainty, mistrust, and shattered nerves.

The more serious and original the task, the more tormenting the self-misgiving." What prevents this from becoming a pathology or depressive state is the joyfulness of misgiving, the vigorous (though sometimes manic and debilitating) movement of the soul at play among its form-seeking doubts. If the activity is kept in motion, if the soul doesn't lose its delight in play, the act of misgiving won't become a manner or regnant mood.

⌣

In *The Metamorphoses*, Daedalus warns Icarus to fly a middle course:

> Don't go too low, or water will weigh the wings down;
> Don't go too high, or the sun's fire will burn them.
> Keep to the middle way.

That's the technologue's sound advice to the artist, which the artist has to reject. Typical fatherly advice, too. No wonder poets envy engineers. So much power amassed in the middle, wadded and cunningly balanced there. In one of my favorite Williams poems he complains to a lover that it makes him sick to see how quickly a new bridge gets built while he can't find time to get a book written:

> They have the power,
>
> that's all, she replied. That's what you all
> want. If you can't get it, acknowledge
>
> at least what it is. And they're not
> going to give it to you.

⌣

I meet a famous critical theorist who says when she taught at the University of Iowa students from the Creative Writing Program were among her most clever students. I say that critical theory turns poems into illustrations of ideas, a verbal equivalent of conceptual art. The usefulness of theory lies in its skepticism, its refusal to let old ways of thinking pass unquestioned, challenging poetry, painting, and ideology whenever they begin to seem (in Iris Murdoch's phrase) "too naively and soothingly referential." Poetry may question the nature of reality, but I think it mostly wants to express the feeling of putting such questions and of living with that uncertainty.

⌒

On being a nobody. What if books of poetry were published according to the Barnes principle? In the Barnes Foundation, the pictures have no wall labels identifying artist, title, date, style, etc. A single artist's works aren't grouped together but deployed among others. I imagine books of poetry made available to the public without illustrious dust jackets, blurbs, bios, medals of merit embossed on the cover, hysterical reviews, etc. That way, everybody becomes a nobody, except for the singularity and expressiveness of the offering in the words. What if books of poems were, as a recent Nobel Laureate has proposed, displayed at supermarket checkout counters? Yes, but let them be displayed anonymously, in plain wrappers. Browse and shop, shop and buy, yes? Let the poet who suggested that, and the poet suggesting this, be the first to have their works so displayed.

⌒

A bit from Louise Bogan's more or less autobiography, *Journey Around My Room*: "The light on leaves in the evening looked as though it did not come from the sun, but from space itself, or from some element in a universe so distant from our own that it must be felt, never seen, and never named." And this: "Long continued pain reduces one to the state of a blustering child, or exacerbates one into an arrogant tyrant. Either 'I can't bear this; help me' (with tears); or 'I'm bearing this and don't you for a moment forget it'." It's one of the most beautiful deployments of self-exposure of any of our poets. Her prose has the lyric signature of her poetry. Her mind had an economy of passion, a compactness, and tartness. Every word in the journals seems put there, placed with pursed deliberateness, very little that's casual, whimsical, accidental.

﹏

So much pressure from universities, mass media, photography, painting, etc. to be conceptual, theoretical, diagnostic. An idea of an artwork suffices to make something, anything, so. How many poems now are more or less ideas or conceptualizations of poems? Better to be expressive, front and center, blatant, rude.

﹏

Only in early middle age can one cross over into the country of *amor fati*—Dante's *Commedia* is the longest deposition on this—as something more than a literary or philosophical notion. *Amor fati* isn't resignation, it's something achieved. So, consider a nation abiding by *amor fati*, love fate so that you'd be willing to relive your life exactly as you've already lived it. So, there's been hard rain for days now, and the mangy dogs of the media, for lack of anything better to do, are tearing off pieces of Obama's flesh. We live in such a culture of the obscene—splashed daily on TV cable news, on YouTube, etc.—that it's risible to hear people speak of the seven-figure salaries of bankers, hedge fund managers, and auto executives as "obscene." "Fail better, fail bigger" is a requisite of capitalist success. That's not obscene, it's Puritan. The USA loves to reward failure so long as greed and grotesque sums are at stake. "Show me the way to the next whiskey bar, / O don't ask why." The USA abhors the poor because they're perceived as morally defective. Greed is our national Jungian shadow. *Nobody* is innocent, including those suffering persons who expected a huge something (house) for a little nothing (no-down payment subprime loans). The first varmints to be shot, though, should be the indiscriminate predators.

﹏

Ruskin in his great autobiography, *Praeterita*: "Accuracy of diction means accuracy of sensation, and precision of accent, precision of feeling."

Coleridge's letter to the Wordsworth household in which he confesses to "sinkings and misgivings, alienations from the Spirit of Hope, obscure withdrawings out of life . . . a wish to retire into stoniness and to stir not, or to be diffused upon the winds & have no individual existence." The melancholic's self-abnegation. But that's just half the cycle. In my life it's not stoniness but muddiness, rubbery, dense, adhesive, impossible to rise from. The other part of the cycle is wild pushy uncontrollable activity, speed babble. A helium delight in the smallest tickings of daily life, the sick excitement of staying in motion and keeping the things of the world in motion around me.

No wonder I'm so fond of San Francisco and Bologna and their curved topographies sloping or arcing or radiating from epicenters. Growing up in Philadelphia, my geographical imagination had no curves. When I looked at maps, at the lush, gibbous forms of Africa and South America, the fleshy pendant of Florida, the floating debris of South Sea Islands, in my mind's eye they somehow turned into the Philadelphia street plan—grids, equidistant streets, rule-edged north by south and east by west, the rubbery staves of power lines over trackless trolleys, the gleaming steel streetcar rails. On Sunday visits to my aunts' houses in North Philadelphia we drove seven miles straight up Broad Street, with only the curlicue around City Hall to interrupt that Puritan pursuit. When I finally left the city, I wanted only roundings and spirals and elevations and pitches—a flexing line extending infinitely in space.

Cindy Sherman's pictures of dummies, anatomical models from medical supply stores, splayed on their backs, twisted or hitched up on all fours, rear ends pedantically displayed, nightmarishly oversized detachable vulvas and penises. In a few, Sherman's head, bewigged and made-up like a "painted woman," looks screwed to the top of a dummy body, or balanced there like a lightbulb in a shooting gallery. She makes the body look like a prosthesis of consciousness. Her art watches us as we watch it. It's moral surveillance, vigilante art, fish-eyed, taunting. I always feel a little ashamed of candor about the body when I look at her pictures. They're meant to intensify self-consciousness in that way, but they're also chastising and abstract. She vaguely scolds, in a haunted or gleeful way, about not thinking enough about how we think about the body. So much thinking about the body is enough already! How much self-consciousness and diagnosis can any artist tolerate before self-consciousness inflects primary feeling out of existence?

⁓

I'll never get used to it, living in Redwood City, this suburb on the West Coast's brittle crust, migrating once or twice a year to my old South Philadelphia neighborhood and its tumultuous seasons. Here: sunshine, earthquake weather, cheaply constructed and ludicrously expensive houses, dense racial and ethnic mix, Spanish spoken everywhere. There: redbrick houses fastidiously kept and tackily decorated by Italian Americans who speak no Italian but for bursts of dialect. I feel my soul has dropped into a cyberspace that blends those different structures, weathers, languages—the brown beaches of Atlantic City and the momentous closed faces of the casinos standing watch; the crumbling cliffs of the West Coast with its sea lions and gray whales. One March, in Philadelphia, a great thunderstorm comes up. Purple sky, buds gleaming on dark trees. Lightning filaments split the sky in the chutes between skyscrapers, then the rain falls hard and heavy. But it's also something that, pouring down on me, shuts me out.

⁓

The sacred doesn't require of us affirmation so much as pursuit of what we humanly are, full of conflict and uncertainty. Poetry is possessed of some quality of the sacred when the patterns of its words embody the vitality of contradiction and strife. I sense the presence of the sacred most intensely when I'm most in conflict with myself.

⌣

The mystery of details. We enter a familiar gallery and go at once (or pretend to drift) to a favorite picture, because it has a detail we love, as we love lines or phrases in poems we hardly remember the entire drift of. In the Frick I go to the Vermeer with the cavalier wearing a big black hat. I go for the hat, it's a topography, a landscape of fashion. Black of black, it determines the space in the painting and, strangely, makes for the intensest gaiety. In the Philadelphia Museum of Art, agitated by all the reminders of why I had to leave South Philly so many years ago, I go to images that call me back to myself. Vitale da Bologna's little busybody *Crucifixion*. And Cézanne's *Large Bathers*, where the life of flesh is made to seem sensuously complete in a landscape magisterially unfinished. And the small self-portrait of a very youthful Tintoretto—it has the intensity of gaze that later made his pictures of sacred events so disturbing; but the really great thing in the portrait is his ear, painted with a freedom and casual enthusiasm that I love. An artist's concentration is such that certain details will suddenly bear, unexpectedly, a full sense of existence. A hat, an ear, a phrase.

⌣

The things of the world, their chancy stirrings, all in motion, as the Soul is in motion in the world. At certain moments there comes a fused presence of times and things, stopped, as if on view before the Soul, staged there, while the Soul continues to move, too, before and around the vision. In a North Beach coffee shop, trying to concentrate on a book, the taste of the coffee distracts me, and the perspective of my view from the window seat, down the sidewalk and toward the unseen Bay, takes me out of myself. Like a transparency, the scene becomes one where I'm at a bar in my other favorite city, Bologna, twenty years ago. Such different places—hilly, fogswept, sunny, open-faced San Francisco; recondite, medieval, porticoed, noble Bologna. The likes and unlikes all at once come together as one sensation. I've just read in my book: "Against whom do we struggle if not against our own double? Against that *other* in us who would have us believe that the world is without meaning?" The words are Bonnefoy's, the book a gift from E., who inscribed it to me, "who has something in common with this French poet." (But what, exactly?) The Soul turns and stirs not to keep the *other* away but to engage it in conversation, in the motion of words and statements. Behind or above Bonnefoy's words are the waitresses' voices, Italian voices saying something about Santa Maria, just as church bells start to strike. The bells toll in three-strike clusters, tentative almost, as if belief were now an iffy thing, but then finally with a satisfying, resolute balance and completion. What is this joy, so irrational and plain it makes me weep, to be here with these words of book and voice with the taste of the cities and the sound of the bells? Time feels like a substance, a liquid coming into crystal, but it's also a shadow, quickened, porous, unresistant, made of wind and light. The whole of it is what is merely given.

⌣

Labor Day, 1993. I go walking early evening in the park down my suburban street. Two Little League diamonds, soccer field, softball fields, kiddie area. My neighborhood each year draws more immigrants, from Mexico, Salvador, Fiji Islands, India. As I walked in the almost dark I was drawn by the sounds of voices singing sweetly but not harmoniously. A dozen or so Islanders, more or less mournful and more or less drunk, were singing songs of their country. Soon they were serenading me and the young family that had stopped to listen. A sad song, it seemed, but sung with some melancholy joy of remembrance. When I go to teach at the university, I go to the Land of Abstraction, where I overhear theories about marginalized peoples, privileged texts and discourses, hegemonies and heterodoxies. I try to read an essay by a Latina critical theorist who compares her life as a marginalized person in the university to the station of domestic servants, yard workers, day laborers. She's a full professor at a private university and must earn a good salary. Professional opportunism and the standard-issue obtuseness of the professoriat don't concern me. But what is the work of criticism? Not to practice an elite language and enthrone oneself in the executive manor of unintelligibility. Not to claim to speak for the oppressed while using a language of the oppressor. It is somehow to listen to woozy singing in a park and answer it with equivalent plain intensity. The work of criticism ought to be to absorb and carry on that songfulness.

⁓

Old Italian proverb:

> *L'uccello canta nella gabbia*
> *Non di gioia ma di rabbia!*

> The songbird in its cage
> Sings not for joy, but rage!

From the 1980s

In grade school, in the 1950s, once every two weeks the good sister would pass out Picture Study books, thin but mysteriously weighty pamphlets covered in heavy brown paper. Inside were small color reproductions of masterpieces approved by the diocese for eight-year-old minds. It was always a great moment, not for the rarity of the experience, though that was true enough in a culture where the only images on walls in most houses were devotional ones (and where there were few books). But rather for the way so much hard, clear fact could be presented, pictured, in a way that seemed to transcend fact. The colors in the images were so much beyond what I knew that they seemed sacramental. Even now, when I look at a painting by Millet I can't separate from my judgment the feelings rooted in Picture Study time, when *The Gleaners, The Sower,* and *The Angelus* were dominant images. It's not nostalgia. Those pictures were turbulent experiences that ripped me from my familiar world. Though they weren't far from devotional images, they showed great passion for the world of sensation and force. I'm moved in similar ways, and my judgment riddled, when I look at Courbet or Van Gogh, because of their coincidence, secular and religious, with Millet. In Van Gogh I always see devotional mania—sacrificial, elemental, pious. When I look at Matisse's *The Red Studio,* or the Cézanne *Bathers* in the Philadelphia Museum of Art, or Pollock's *Autumn Rhythm (Number 30),* it's the Picture Study child in me that first cries to them.

⌣

In a certain Australian tribe, boys about to be initiated are taken from their mothers by fierce masked men who carry them outside the village, make them lie on the ground, then cover them entirely with sticks and branches. They are "buried" in order to create an artificial night, an "underground," estranged from the familiar night with stars and moon. They're interred in that absolute darkness, surrounded by terrifying creatures, until the arrival of the god is signaled by the sound of bull-roarers. These states of being are repeated throughout the initiation period. Removal, burial, darkness and death, terror and the arrival of the god. The forms of poetry in a secular time are like that. In and of nature, they yet are not natural but cultural. That artificial surround, the hermeticism of form, makes you all the more alert to the presence of gods and their terrifying assistants. Unlike the initiate, the poet isn't just the sufferer and receptor, but also the respondent, giving shape to the formless divine darkness. In the sounds of the poem-coming-into-being, you hear and pursue the sound of bull-roarers; the rough music of the poem in its beginnings is the noise of the approaching deity.

⌒

William James, in *The Varieties of Religious Experience*, disguises his own experience in the report of a fictitious Frenchman who during a depressive episode, he's overcome by "a horrible fear of my own existence" and recalls an epileptic he'd seen in an asylum who would sit all day on a bench, knees drawn up to his chin: "He sat there like a sort of sculpted Egyptian or Peruvian mummy, moving nothing but his black eyes and looking absolutely non-human. This image and my fear entered into a species of combination with each other. *That shape am I*, I felt. Potentially nothing that I possess can defend me against that fate, if the hour for it should strike for me as it struck for him."

⌒

The power of second sight possessed by Johnny in the movie *The Dead Zone* is allegorical of the poet's work. His power is conferred, or rather he's delivered unto it, when a car accident puts him into a five-year coma. When he emerges from that chrysalis, he finds that touching a person releases images of peril from that person's past, future, or present. When the hospital nurse checks his pulse, he sees flames in her daughter's bedroom and warns her in time to save the child. Johnny's consciousness becomes host to histories and destinies. His dominant humor is melancholia. Petrarch was a despairing melancholic lifted at times by arbitrary enthusiasms: "I find myself within the borders of two very different peoples from whence I can see both past and future." Ortega sums up his temperament: "Petrarch lived an indecisive life, coming and going from one to the other—*ora guardo davanti, ora guardo addietro.*" The present becomes an impassioned index or mediator or freezer compartment of past and future. Looking ahead, looking backwards, one *sees.*

⌣

I teach, I explain, I talk talk talk. Near the end of term a student asks a question. So I talk and talk, trying to clarify the issue, whatever it is. I feel, as I usually do (awake or dreaming, in a classroom or anywhere else) that I'm failing to express, failing to explain. So I say, "Do you understand what I'm trying to say?" "No," the student answers. "But that's okay. I never understand anything you say."

⌣

You have a dream that wakes you, and in those first opaque streams of consciousness you still see, or aftersee, some piece of the dream (a boot, a bobby pin, the peeled caulking around a door) but the entire structure of the dream stays amorphous, fluid, about to shimmer away, though you know it's *this* integral picture that you need and want to see. The feeling-tone of the dream is all too urgent (you're still crying or giggling or trembling) but you can't see in your mind's eye the whole clear structure that induced the tone. That's what thinking about poetry is like. The dream is the actual writing of the poem.

⌣

Sometimes objects become grotesquely magnified or distorted. Buildings look taller, plumper, literally stuffed with things and people. Everyday things—a pen or spoon, cigarette, button, doorknob—become elastic and swell or bloat. Faces of strangers and friends bulge and shine with some grave inner light. Then comes the pulsing at the core of that expansiveness, a quickened over-ripening of things. Surfaces throb. Everything's a commonplace fever dream. Yesterday, in a meadow, under a hot midsummer sun, it was a gigantic bumblebee working the crocus.

⌣

Baudelaire says, "*Tout ce qui n'est pas sublime est inutile et coupable*"—"All that falls short of the sublime is useless and reprehensible." Not the sort of idea any gallery dealer or publisher can entertain. And it's an idea that artists redefine in their work. Baudelaire didn't know he was practically at the threshhold of Impressionism and would have been appalled by the new attempt to master sensation induced by nature's momentary appearances, modernism's recasting of the sublime.

⌣

Van Gogh's famous simplicity—his sister refers to it repeatedly in her memoir—jumps from his letters with rude directness and ingenuousness: "The world only concerns me in so far as I feel a certain debt and duty towards it because I have walked that earth for thirty years, and, out of gratitude, want to leave some souvenir in the shape of drawings or pictures" (August 1883). His work wasn't a specialized or sectarian activity, it wasn't a secular profession, it was the fluid, harmonious expression of an existence, and it took as its subject the fullness of existence. Art doesn't redeem experience or set itself at some invulnerable, ironic remove. Maybe this explains why the action in his landscapes coils and oscillates toward convergences, the impossible point of Oneness. His cypress trees, compacted and wrapped in their protoplasmic energy, convulsively shear away toward the ether, toward a bonding with nature's other elements. His painterly gestures were acts of fanatical reciprocity.

⌣

What does a poet want?

—The thing-life of paint, its immediate presence of image, without giving up the pure thought-life of words.

⌣

In the 1850s Millet wrote, "Nature yields herself to those who trouble to explore her, but she demands an exclusive love. The works of art we love, we love only because they are derived from her. The rest are merely works of empty pedantry." That describes Van Gogh's devotionalism, though it wasn't only created nature he explored and loved in that way. The force of space, the throbbing channels and fibers of household objects, are palpable even in his interiors. A floor, a bed, a table, a vase, a wall, even "denatured" stuff quivered with a divinity that for him lived in matter. He paints stars not as distant objects moving away from us, whose light always arrives so late, but as immanent presences, stirrings in consciousness. He narrates the ancient fact that the stars are divine beings. The firmament covered the walls of his most impoverished rooms.

⌣

I love Courbet's drawing *Seated Model Reading in the Studio*. How supple and thoughtless she is, slouching, apparently unawares, a little distracted by what she's reading in her book. Another mood, violently different, is struck in his *Still Life with Apples, Pears, and Pomegranates*. The teeming internal force of the pomegranates thins out the rind and makes it shine with fever-dream vibrance; they are full of some rage of nature, something left of Persephone's appetite, her passion and its consequences in the underworld. Courbet's realism is life lived twice, in the sensuous solidity of actual appearances and in the myth that memorializes it in another present.

⌣

In the dream, I'm with my wife by a river that's nearly in flood, running high and also twisting wildly against its current. (It reminds me of Stubbs's horse twisting toward the lion on its back.) She leaves, urging me to follow, but I lag behind, watching the torrent, and I realize I'm actually looking into the form of the river. The churning and heaving disintegrate into thousands of perfectly enunciated—the forms I'm seeing have the force of speech—loops, curlicues, waves, spirals. In that same instant I know I'm looking into Van Gogh's late paintings, into *Crows Over a Wheat Field* and *Cypresses*. I see into the vitality of the pattern—each brushstroke, each small action of the water, pulses like an artery. My dream recognition, that natural force finds its completest imitation in art, wakes me into tremendous sadness.

⌣

"But consciousness," Jung says, "continually in danger of being led astray by its own light and of becoming a rootless will o' the wisp, longs for the healing power of nature, for the deep wells of being and for unconscious communion with life in all its countless forms."

⌣

Keats had the most urgently self-corrective, self-adjustive mind among the great poets of his time. The reflectiveness became a style in the odes, and it speaks for the remarkable wholeness of his life, the continuity between mental quality and the formalizing of it in poetry. In Coleridge, reflectiveness and self-correctiveness became a paralyzing scrupulosity, maybe because he was *turned* toward speculative philosophy as a means of expression while Keats was turned entirely toward expression in the forms of poetry.

⌣

You look at a hundred good pictures, then one begins to teach you all over again how to see, like Degas' sketch of a dancer, *essence* on a hot green ground of wove paper. Her tutu is just a zigzag gesture, the lower leg extended from that green, growing out of the color, defined only by a minimal outline of skirt. The mark makes the field of force. It's an image of retinal impression re-emergent from memory—an act of exuberant, urgent recovery. In the 1890s Degas's eyesight was going. He told a young painter: "It's all very well to copy what you see, but it's better to draw what you see in your mind. . . . Then your memory and imagination are freed from the tyranny imposed by nature."

⌒

Artists who take their Americanness too literally as a subject are likely to become just processors of American facts, though in the bargain they may also become well known (and prosperous) producers of such facts as commodities.

⌒

Is it worth the effort to perfect a rhetoric of coy but conquering persuasion that mocks its own intentions? Is it worth the effort to make oneself—painter or poet—a genius of affected affectlessness. *That* is the most disconcerting sentimentality of our time. We've come so far from Bergson, who less than a century ago could say that the universe is a machine for the making of gods!

⌒

Van Gogh writing to Theo from Arles in 1888: "I can very well do without God both in my life and in my painting, but I cannot, ill as I am, do without something which is greater than I, which is my life—my power to create." He could do without God but not transcendence. What is that greater "something?" I think it is the consciousness that may be entirely one's own but which the artist, any artist, experiences and exercises as greater and more inclusive than his own. That's how its reality is felt in one's working moments. It frees the artist into fearlessness and formal impiety.

⌒

Lesser art doesn't challenge itself, doesn't become adversarial; it can only breed its own unquestioned, and sometimes quite moving, perfections. It's singular and meticulously idiosyncratic. It presents itself as what its time wants, not what it needs.

⌐

With collage the modern artist became an archivist of the actual, taking message bearers, prescriptive signs of all sorts—labels, newspaper clips, menus, printouts—and slanting them into defiantly non-prescriptive fields. Private language redeems public debris, signs saved to be made over into another existence. The master image becomes an archeological site seeded by the artist. The recovery of visual fact is fused in a figure-ground relation with oblivion. Collage thrives especially in a culture that can easily imagine its own ruins.

⌐

A frequent childhood dream was of blocky masses of spongy gray-white vapors. They terrified me because they could possess me, absorb me into their mass, though that also felt inviting, even desirable, a return to pure, undifferentiated beginnings, a flight from the pains of unlikeness. When I first looked at Rothko's paintings in the 1970s I was moved in ways I couldn't understand or articulate. Something in them exercised what Lawrence calls "the insidious mastery of song." Their claim had to do with that old dream of mine and also the paintings' non-anecdotal quality: the abandonment of narrative, of figurative and scenic suggestiveness, became a dense presence, a sumptuous forfeiture.

⌐

In his chapter on Leonardo in *The Renaissance*, Pater writes, "The way to perfection is through a series of disgusts." For moderns, the way matters more than the perfection, and the disgusts themselves are exemplary.

What Yeats called "personality" was important to him in the 1920s, but for him personality was ritualized and externalized as Mask. It wasn't what we normally mean by it, viz., personhood, the "natural" quality or character of the person in the poem, a person that practices a companionable sort of benign self-absorption. In our talk about poetry we usually mean the opposite of Yeats's self-conscious ceremonialism. Our assumptions are more Victorian; we tend to identify the moral quality of a poem with the moral quality of the person detectable in the poem.

It's a casual fearlessness to live the moment unawares, to sleep heedless as we do, sometimes in each other's arms, visited and scared by a past we didn't know we made or experienced, the plummy bleeding images of tundra, purple parakeets, Grandpop costumed in his coffin like the Queen of Hearts, then you wake to recall the pot-au-feu sent back to the kitchen. We're in that instant of shared out-of-time time and in the instant itself. The ceiling fans tamper finely with the lamplight, unknown voices hug the walls, closer now to us in this peculiar solitude of two that we compose and feel at home in. The flowers her lover sent boisterous behind the bar, and we know that this is, all of it, nothing of consequence yet full of itself and full of us.

From the shadows falling among the eucalyptus trees where I like to walk, on the same wind that carries that healing scent comes the hurt, dignified cry of bagpipe music, played by a woman on a small path, by her car, alone, treading almost motionless between the long shadows in slow time to that cry, her step measured by no cadence I can hear. It's as if she stopped of a sudden, stepped from the car, and began to play. It's a call.

In his essay on Goethe, Ortega writes: "Every life is, more or less, a ruin among whose debris we have to discover what the person ought to have been." What, then, if that person in life consciously designs that ruin, almost as a mock ruin or diorama? That ruin is already, in life, a "set piece." What interpretive record can there be of such a life?

—⌣—

Not so! I've now heard that bagpipe music on other days, in other moods, but always in the same place, under the eucalyptus, and she walks the same path, keeps close to her car. The call becomes habit.

—⌣—

In *Art and Anarchy*, Edgar Wind discusses Giovanni Morelli's argument for making correct attributions. "This is the core of Morelli's argument: an artist's personal instinct for form will appear at its purest in the least significant parts of his work, because they are the least labored." Say the same about a poet's work. What can be felt in the simplest, least significant turn of phrase is the stirring of language in answer to the poet's instinct for the necessary form. A poet follows the pattern that language generates the way a painter follows or pursues the emergent image. It's the strange perfume of the work.

—⌣—

What's really useful? Perry Miller's description of Jonathan Edwards: "He was passionately interested in experience, his own, his wife's, his people's—or the universe's—because in experience was to be detected the subtle working of the pattern; but he was supremely uninterested in personality, his own or anybody else's. Especially, we may add, his own." I want a poetry of that kind of experience, not poetry that lives by the quality of the idiosyncratic person made present in the poem. I want to be caught up by the inwardings of experience, by what William James calls that strung-along sort of flowing reality of consciousness.

We say something is "the worst" to persuade ourselves of the power and force of the happening, that it's the new extremest measure, and to dignify the suffering the event brings us. When really we can only speak of present ills as something "worse" than what once was. "Worst" is a future idea, a future passion. We say "worst" because we have to believe there's a limit to the pain and that we have, luckily, already achieved it, touched it. It's a promise to ourselves that nothing worse can happen now.

Reading Malory. The character of the lyric poet, expressed in Lancelot's first question to the unknown damsel he meets in the forest after a long journey: "Fayre damesel, know ye in this contrey ony adventures nere hande?"

To borrow Francis Bacon's method? After finishing a painting he swipes a section of the canvas with rag or sponge then leaves it, abandons it. A willed arbitrariness, the tight little delirium of messing up forms achieved through toil, the violence to *derange* the figure into new meaning, formlessness integral to the form. It's a matter of letting instinct mess with things once the form of the poem has already begun to "set." To encourage the strange word-traces of the dream life, invasive scenic oddnesses, mistakes—let them decide the poem's form.

From the Taoist Kuan Tzu text (330 BC): "The earth is the origin of all things, the nest and the garden of all life. . . . Water is the blood and breath of the earth, flowing and communicating within its body as if in sinews and veins." Therefore poison the blood, foul the nest, scatter filth in the garden, as a promise to our children.

Therefore profit. Progress, human industry, the supremacy of the technological imagination.

⌣

We live most fully in the present when we're in pain. The past becomes a block of useless rubble recognizable only because it's a monument to a time when pain was not. It's a ruined Eden. The future is imaginable only as oblivion—of pain, of ourselves. There's no reach or stretch of time called "future," there's only "the end of pain," a deliverance. Then, afterward—the future might begin again, later on.

⌣

Keats's remark about Negative Capability has become a literary cult object. Some use it to justify ignorance—embrace doubt and uncertainty, for it will do you good. But we travesty Keats's inquiring, sensuous intelligence if we think he's endorsing the unwillingness to pass judgment, evaluate, assert, deny. Negative Capability is not counsel for failed nerve. Keats was advising himself to be patient in the quest for definitiveness. It's the counsel of patience of the imagination.

⌣

A devastating, impious assumption that the world in all its hard bright particulars exists so that we can write poems about it. (Or that it exists by virtue of language's capacity to make statements about it.)

⌣

Public culture is obligated to ennoble the trivial. That's its function in an industrial democracy. It happens at all levels—TV, pop music, book and magazine publishing. Democracy assumes that even what's mediocre or undistinguished can (or must) be elevated, exalted, in service of individual genius.

Humans have probably always written or spoken or sung or coughed up poetry or chants or songs. Its beauty had use and was folded into religious activity. Cave painting must have happened during some vocalization of the powers registered in the paintings, repetitive and religious songs meant to summon and control relations between humans, the animals they hunted, and the powers that guided and destined the hunt. Poetry preserved and continued communal consciousness. That impulse hasn't died, but the desire has thinned out.

⌣

William James is representative of the American poet, barging and sweet-talking and singing disturbing songs through an American here-and-now with the accumulated stuff of Western Europe right there at his back. From a manuscript page of *The Varieties of Religious Experience*: "It comes home to one only at particular times. . . . The more original religious life is always lyric—'the monk owns nothing but his lyre'—and its essence is to dip into another kingdom, to feel an invisible order." To tell the feeling of that invisible order, to tell the felt sense of its presence or evanescence, is a proper ambition for an American poet.

⌣

Rain, snow, fog, lightning. In the coal grate Coleridge sees "the stranger," that film of flame, and says, "its puny flaps and freaks the idling Spirit / By its own moods interprets." It's a passive gesture, then, this determination-by-association? The spirit must be at rest, sleepy, vulnerable, suggestible. Only then can it have a sharper recognition of reality. And what it recognizes is consciousness going about its business of subjectivity. What matters is the precision of the report, and the authenticity of the feeling.

⌣

79

Public literary culture in America: a buffalo carcass around which buzz hundreds of fat flies. Then come the larger carrion feeders. From a distance it looks like a great festive occasion. All that activity and titillating buzzing. All that ripe rich color.

⌣

William Carlos Williams, looking middle-aged as he does in most photographs. But I'm watching his hands, the most beautifully formed hands I've ever seen, slender but powerfully muscled, and they shine with some inner light. Out of nowhere he takes a small, brightly furred creature in his hands and begins to tell me about its vitality, its life principle. As he speaks, his fingers press gently into the animal's fur and begin to dig into the skin, slowly prizing the animal apart like a peach or fig until its inners are visible. Holding the torn, still squirming creature, he exposes, then strokes and prods, the feathery white muscle tissue, explaining that the animal's strength and agility—its *power*—is due to these unseen structures.

⌣

I don't feel that I lost my faith; I feel I've fallen from or out of belief, as if it were a terrace in the mind. The falling is a negative condition, zero minus something. You never hit bottom, you just keep falling and get accustomed to that downwarding.

⌣

Schiller's advice in *On the Aesthetic Education of Man*: "Live with your century, but do not be its creature; render to your contemporaries what they need, not what they praise."

⌣

I go walking in the hills early morning with my poet friend R. We see a few mule deer grazing in a clearing, a tarantula crossing the road, white spiders and their larvae on some devilish thistle, and a bobcat. Bobcats prefer to hunt in heavy brush, but this one was in the open, crossing a large meadow drilled all over by ground squirrels that had left piles of dirt everywhere. The bobcat paused over a burrow, held still for a few minutes, and in a sudden blur held a flapping squirrel in its mouth. It looked at us then turned and walked back into the woods. R later said how the event begged for a response, an answering poem. That if he brooded long enough it might yield something. We argued, because I'm skeptical, too skeptical for my own good, of charged opportune occasions. (Experience anyway takes a long time to settle in me before I can bring it over into poetry.) Poetry answers to the world's occasions, and attention to that reciprocal relation is the important work of self-preparation, of readiness. And yet I feel ill-prepared and reluctant when an occasion seems too opportune, as if reality were presenting me with homework. The force of revelation for me is a gradual thing, not a sudden strike or cracking open of a chrysalis. Revelation comes when I'm able and prepared to watch and testify to the moral relations of the world. The relations matter more than melodramatic event. Revelation is serial recognition. I realized later that R and I were in fact caught up in the nature of the offering—the morning light, the fragrance of bay laurel, the little powdery detonations in the field, the coming and going of the bobcat—and the *duty* we both felt to recognize it. The world's circumstance and chance had offered this to us. What could we offer in reply? Words that remake and restore the occasion? Words that preserve the image of the time? Or that invoke the god in the scene?

⌣

One of Darwin's facts, reported in *The Voyage of the Beagle*: "Certainly no fact in the long history of the world is so startling as the wide and repeated extermination of its inhabitants."

⌣

A Sioux who fought at Little Bighorn later said that the soldiers carried lots of money, which he and other braves stripped from the bodies. They knew what the silver was but not the greenbacks.

The children played with these, made tepees out of them, gathered dozens of bills which they stuck together to make toy shawls, though much of the money was stained with blood.

⌣

I told myself that hearing Mass after nearly fifteen years would be merely a kind of social call. But what moved me about the ceremony (did I expect not to be moved? did I expect to stop falling?) was so different from what used to pulse inside me all those years ago. It seemed no longer a ritual loaded with grace, but a volatility, a faith burnt up and renewed with each gesture, each word, resolving moment to moment into divine power incarnated then dissipated, the awful glory of the dying man-god. Maybe one has to fall first, and keep falling, to feel that quickened glee of divine immanence, and to know—*to feel along the heart*—the terror of the story of the god that visits mortals who kill him, and who after being shut inside the earth returns to the sky, some Elsewhere. Calling himself, in the flesh, back from death, he explodes the vessel of earth, melts the stone, leaving behind a message, some stories, a precipice of belief. (The woman's first thought when she finds the tomb empty—the Caravaggio angel standing angry by the tomb knows no one will understand what he has to say and doesn't much care—is that somebody has *stolen* the human god.) Nietzsche was the purest and in his way most pious anti-Christian in insisting that one must live wholly and entirely in this webwork of human existence. There can be no imagined, obliging transcendent Other which offers promise of another life. I can't begin to understand the happiness of those who rest content in one view or the other. My relation to the imagination of the divine is always an ambiguity, a struggle of self-definition.

⌣

A show by a local artist ran for weeks at a Virginia gallery but nothing sold. On one of his discouraging reconnoiters, in a rage of disappointment he started screaming at visitors then took a can of spray paint and—like Baptiste in *Children of Paradise* when he scribbles greasepaint on his image in a mirror—sprayed an enormous X on every picture, threw down the can, and left. A few witnesses asked the dealer about the freshly x-ed out canvases. Word spread. Within a week more than half the paintings sold. He cashed out at around $20,000. The paintings depicted cheesy Southern subjects—plantation homes, magnolia groves, benevolent darkies. Once x-ed out they became ironical, postmodern. The buyers were buying anecdote, something to remind them (ironically) of an actual occurrence of human anguish. The anecdote was the "life art" of the otherwise dead-duck paintings. It had to do with the public's desire to appropriate some expression of real life and passion. They wanted their stories, their lives, to flow briefly through that of the artist's, as if to say there really is some connection, something binding one to another. Save us, again and again, from our singleness!

—⌣—

Dante's invocation at the beginning of *Inferno XXXII*—"*sì che dal fatto il dir non sia diverso*" ("so that the telling will be no different from the fact"). It's important to him to represent exactly the data of vision, the facts of the imagination. To take on the obligation of rendering the clarity of the details the poet fabricates in memory—that's still poetry's moral obligation.

—⌣—

For days you feel turned inside out, as if the nervous system were lining of the flesh's fabric, now all exposed. Whatever's *out there* chafes and grinds. Words, the air, the sound of leaves blown across the pavement. These become desire's claims.

—⌣—

Those mysterious lines that feel delivered, dictated by something greater and other than me. They're a sort of neurogram, a way of writing a condition of nerves governed by a power now unremembered but still active. At the moment of writing, of receiving, the nerves are exposed, the body pulled inside out. The external world registers immediately its painful charge on all the impulses, relays, sortings, resolutions, rearrangements—all the surging neural energy of consciousness.

Postscript

I've kept notebooks since I started writing. They relieved, but also tightened up, the loneliness of the work. They were roomy, shapeless spaces where I could examine and question the intensities I felt toward life and writing. I recorded commonplaces, I argued with them, I recorded life experiences and picked at their meanings, I indulged in irresoluteness and ambiguity and confusion. I started in the 1970s, when I was in my twenties. I was moving around in those days so notebooks went missing, and some of what's left of those years strikes me as juvenilia, so nothing from that period appears here. By the early 1980s I'd become aware that the notes were giving shape and voice to my aspirations and my reckonings with artists—poets and visual artists especially—who mattered to me.

I responded to what I sensed was going on in the public life of poetry, in my private life of poetry, and in the changing neighborhoods of my personal circumstances. The contents became more and more a proofing or filling out of questions I was writing about in other prose—literary essays, art criticism, accounts of life experience. When I published my first collection of essays in 1989, I picked fruits and nuts from the notebooks and made space for them under the heading "Out of Notebooks." The tipsiness and non-consecutiveness of the materials were satisfying to me and gave me a break from the formal demands of the essays.

So I kept doing it. By the late 1980s I'd made myself into an art writer and produced a book of essays, *Out of Eden*, entirely about the visual arts. My notebooks were naturally filling up with that preoccupation, so in *Out of Eden* I included excerpts under the heading "Miscellany." And in my next book of essays, *Shooting the Works: On Poetry and Pictures*, I included more "Out of Notebooks." By that time, 1996, the notebooks had become my workshop, interrogation room, monk's cell. Since then, material that I roughed out in notes have become essays long or short (like "Table Talk" pieces that Wendy Lesser has published in *Threepenny Review*), and after the turn of the century I kept testing what an essay could be. I sometimes took seemingly unrelated passages from the notebooks and treated them as discrete essay components, then published those weirdly constellated chunks—I thought of them as space debris—as out-of-joint essays.

What I've tried to do here is use the notes to craft a shadow self-portrait composed of hopped-up episodes from my mental and emotional life. The notes are saturated with wherever I was writing them. The places, I hope, are self-evident: South Philadelphia, where I lived my first 21 years; San Francisco, where I've spent most of my adult life; the suburbs south of San Francisco, especially Redwood City; Bologna; Chicago. I've always had a mass of material to select from; when I was selecting for the books, I picked what was most related to whatever my obsessions then were. For this here book I picked notes having to do with matters I still go round and round and that still lose me sleep, which accounts for the heavier presence of 2000s material, especially stuff about the jerky dance my dream life and my waking physical and mental itchers and aggravators make together. The entries are undated floaters; that's how they come into and live in my consciousness—much of the time they aren't dated in the original notebooks—except for the rare occasion when a Friday the 13th or New Year's Day or Ash Wednesday has ritualistic significance.

Life overtakes and outruns things anyway, and now with all the recording and receiving and transmitting surfaces of digital technology, cultures in most places get breathless (or nauseated) trying to keep up with the present. My notebooks, if nothing else, give a sense of what it's like trying to keep up with the past. I haven't updated facts as they originally appeared. The Barnes Foundation [p. 54] I write of, for instance, is now its own museum in Philadelphia, and the superb stone elephants of Bologna's Palazzo degli elefanti [p. 43] may by now be planed flat by urban erosions, or restored.